FOR THE LOVE OF
SCOTLAND

A COMPANION

NORMAN FERGUSON

summersdale

FOR THE LOVE OF SCOTLAND

Summersdale Publishers Ltd
46 West Street
Chichester
West Sussex
PO19 1RP
UK

www.summersdale.com

Printed and bound in the Czech Republic

ISBN: 978-1-78685-052-2

Substantial discounts on bulk quantities of Summersdale books are available to corporations, professional associations and other organisations. For details contact general enquiries: telephone: +44 (0) 1243 771107, fax: +44 (0) 1243 786300 or email: enquiries@summersdale.com.

This book, designed by
William B. Taylor
is a production of
Edito-Service S.A., Geneva

Printed in Switzerland

CONTENTS

INTRODUCTION

During the first years of the third millennium, those in charge of running Scotland created a slogan to help promote tourism and attract investment. It said Scotland was 'the best small country in the world'. This claim was not hugely popular with Scots – it didn't sit right. The aims were fine: a publicly shown pride in the nation and its achievements, but it just wasn't very Scottish. Scots are not very good at showing off; they're not encouraged to boast of their achievements, no matter how great. If they do, they face being brought down to earth with the withering comment 'I kent his faither' (I knew his father – who does he think he is?).

Modern-day Scotland retains a large degree of myth and romanticism – for the first, none comes bigger than the large aquatic creature that lives in Loch Ness, and for the latter, the 1981 film *Gregory's Girl* made the breeze-block uniformity of new town Cumbernauld the most romantic place in the world.

Scotland is lucky to have symbols easily recognisable in the global community. There are often complaints about using tartan, mountains, lochs and whisky in promoting Scotland, but they are now an essential part of Scotland's identity.

I was born and grew up in Scotland and have lived in half of the major cities, as well as some of the rural areas, and over the years I've accumulated many facts and stories that I hope will be of interest. For a country as small as it is (although it makes up a third of the UK's land mass) it has packed in a lot of history.

This book hopes to highlight the major events, people, landscapes, culture, scientific achievements and sporting moments of glory that have been celebrated over the centuries since the Romans made the first recorded notes of the 'Scotti', who lived north of Hadrian's Wall. The weather also features…

I hope you will find much of interest in these pages and that the book is – as the Scottish phrase says – 'better than a slater up your nose'.*

Norman Ferguson
May 2017

---

* A better situation than having a woodlouse in your nasal cavity.

OVERVIEW

Scotland is many things to many people: be it the grandeur of the dramatic Highland landscape of Rob Roy and the clans; the gentle whimsy of the Outer Hebrides as seen in films such as *Whisky Galore!*; or the smoke-covered mills and factories of the Industrial Revolution. It is, of course, all these things and more. And what of those who live here? What is a Scot? The cautious farmer living on the land of his forebears? The gallus Glaswegian taking no nonsense from nobody? The literate and urbane global citizen who can happily spend time up a mountain in Torridon or in a tuk-tuk in Thailand? The stereotypical view of the dry-humoured, quiet, spendthrift Scot who only comes alive after a few drinks does apply to some, of course, but it mostly comes from vaudeville acts of decades ago. The debate about what qualities and attitudes make up the 'typical Scot' could last as long as the Caledonian Canal, and to attempt to pin down an agreed set would be the equivalent of herding wildcats.

Scotland's national motto is *Nemo me impune lacessit* (No one attacks me with impunity) or in Scots: 'Wha daur meddle wi' me?' – which gives some idea of a certain national posture adopted when pressed. Scots take a quiet but stubborn pride in their country, despite numerous setbacks, most notably nowadays in sport, of which more later...

THE PEOPLE

Scots have always looked outside their own borders: to build trading relationships (occasionally to plan military campaigns) and for places to start new lives away from their homeland. Some of those who left for foreign shores – and their descendants – became the most famous of people.

The Scottish language has always been essential in establishing a unique identity for Scots. Furthermore, it is always useful to know if being called a numpty is an insult or a compliment!

LANGUAGE

If you want a linguistic adventure,
go drinking with a Scotsman.
ROBIN WILLIAMS, *LIVE ON BROADWAY*, 2002

Part of the Scottish identity comes through language, which is a mixture that reflects its population's make-up from its early days.

MODERN-DAY LANGUAGES

A mixture of languages are spoken in modern-day Scotland, including Arabic, Bengali, Cantonese, Dutch, English, Farsi, French, Gaelic, German, Hebrew, Hindi, Italian, Japanese, Kurdish, Mandarin, Polish, Punjabi, Scots, Spanish, Turkish and Urdu.

The three main ones are:

Scottish English
English, but spoken with a Scottish accent. Contains Scots words (and occasionally Gaelic).

Scots
Spoken in the north-east and lowlands, Scots includes dialects such as Doric and Lallans. May appear impenetrable to an outsider not familiar with any of the words.

Scottish Gaelic
Similar to Irish Gaelic, it is now mostly spoken in the Highlands and Outer Hebrides, although Gaelic schools have been established in Glasgow and Edinburgh. Gaelic was historically spoken in all parts of Scotland save for the Borders and the north, where Norse was spoken. Around 60,000 Scots can speak Gaelic.

DID YOU KNOW?

The word 'dunce' originates from John Duns Scotus, a philosopher born in 1266, who was from the Borders village of Duns. He was criticised for not being too scholarly in his work.

SCOTS WORDS

The following are Scots words that may already be familiar; but in case they are not, definitions are given:

Bahoochie (n)
The buttocks.

Clipe (n)
A clipe is someone who informs a person in authority of another's bad behaviour, especially in a school environment.

Crabbit (adj)
Grumpy. A crabbit person is one who takes little joy in life and acts as a black hole, drawing in the joie de vivre of others.

Dreich (adj)
A state of grey, dull weather involving cloudiness and low-light levels, where the sun has not been seen for a while. It may also be raining.

Girn (v)
To complain or to whine, like a broken record.

Glaikit (adj)
A person who is glaikit has little chance of winning a Nobel Prize and of whom it may be said 'the lights are on but no one's home'.

Numpty (n)
A person who appears to have low intelligence; an idiot.

Plook (n)
A spot, often seen when a sufferer has acne.

Scunnered (adj)
To be scunnered is to be tired or fed up with a particular aspect of life.

Shooglie (adj)
Something shooglie is something that is unstable. It is used in the expression 'Their jacket is on a shooglie nail' to describe an employee whose long-term future is in doubt.

Stooshie (n)
Similar to a stramash (below).

Stramash (n)
A messy confrontation, often seen in team sports such as junior football or rugby matches.

DID YOU KNOW?

'Blackmail' originates from the Borders, with the word stemming from 'black', indicating a morally suspect deed, and 'mail', being a Scottish word for rent. Cattle stealing was one of the specialities of the infamous Border Reivers – groups that would raid across the border to steal livestock – and tenants would pay them to ensure their cattle and other possessions were not appropriated. The Reivers were around from the Middle Ages to the end of the sixteenth century and resisted overlordship by any king or queen until James VI was able to suppress them permanently.

PHRASES

There are many Scottish phrases that can beautifully and succinctly express a particular emotion or feeling. Here are just some of them:

You're not here to enjoy yourself. (Life on earth is not about pleasure.)

There's nothing easier gotten than a cheat. (Disappointment is easily achieved.)

If brains were dynamite, they couldn't part their hair. (They are short of intelligence.)

They couldn't hit a coo in the erse wi' a banjo. (They're useless when it comes to coordinated effort.)

Back to auld claes and cauld porritch. (Back to old clothes and cold porridge, i.e. the holiday is over and it's time to return to normal life.)

We're all Jock Tamson's bairns. (We're all God's children, i.e. all members of the human race. Jock Tamson is said to have been a church minister in Edinburgh called John Thomson.)

Away an bile yer heid. (You can depart and boil your own head as far as I'm concerned.)

Dae you think my heid's buttoned up the back? (Do you think I am daft?)

They're all fur coat and no drawers. (They're showy with no substance.)

It's better than a slater up your nose. (It's a better situation than having a woodlouse in your nasal cavity.)

You can always tell a Fifer. But not much. (Residents of Fife appear to know a lot.)

They think they're Archie but they're nothing but a flea on Archie's dug. (They have quite a high opinion of themselves but are not really that important.)

That would give your erse a sair heid. (That noise is so bad it would give your backside a headache.)

What's for you won't go past you. (What's fated will happen.)

They've a face like a well-skelped erse. (Their complexion is quite red in colour.)

Lang may your lum reek. (May your chimney smoke for a long time, i.e. may you have a long and happy life.)

DID YOU KNOW?

The phrase 'getting away scot-free' has no connection with Scotland. It means getting away without paying any tax – 'scot' stemming from the word 'shot', a Norse-derived word meaning tax.

IMMIGRATION AND EMIGRATION

Scotland has seen immigration from its very creation, with peoples arriving from all points of the compass. Some, including Saint Columba in the sixth century, brought significant changes to how life was lived, while others arrived, settled and quietly got on with their lives.

Due to the proximity of Scotland and Ireland, it was natural that the inhabitants of both countries would move between the two. The Scots from Ireland arrived in the sixth century and in the seventeenth century King James VI wished to establish a colony on the Emerald Isle. A couple of centuries later, Irish workers made the short crossing over the Irish Sea to work in the industrial central belt. Others have arrived over the years – some from southern Asia and Europe – and have added to the sense of Scotland being a modern country at ease with itself and those who have travelled to live here. Scotland's closest neighbour England has provided the largest group of those choosing to live 'north of the border' over the years.

As well as seeing peoples arrive, Scotland has also had those depart. The Highland clearances are the biggest example of mass migration, with thousands either forced to leave their homes, or doing so voluntarily. Some moved to the central belt while thousands of their countrymen and women boarded ships for Australia, New Zealand, Canada and America. A fifth of people who arrived in New Zealand in the nineteenth century were from Scotland: Dunedin was named after the old name for Edinburgh. In the post-First World War slump of the 1920s, 400,000 more people left Scotland than arrived, and during the 1950s and 1960s another half a million of the population emigrated to other countries. The resulting diaspora, i.e. those who could claim Scottish ancestry, is believed to number up to 40 million around the world.

DID YOU KNOW?

In the late eighteenth century over three-quarters of the men working at the Hudson's Bay Company were from Orkney. They were recruited not just for their hardy nature and ability to thrive in the wild lands of Canada, but also because they were cheaper than men from England and were assumed to be more sober than men from Ireland!

SCOTS ABROAD

There are few more impressive sights
than a Scotsman on the make.
J. M. BARRIE, WHAT EVERY WOMAN KNOWS (1908)

While some carved out quiet lives, and others returned home, there were some Scots abroad who made an impact in their new homelands. Here are some examples:

WILLIAM KIDD (c.1645–1701)
Kidd, the son of a church minister, was from Greenock and became employed by the British government as a privateer. He attacked French settlements in the West Indies before being asked to do the same to pirates in the Indian Ocean. However, he was accused of being one himself and was arrested, tried and hanged in 1701. It is believed that Kidd's lost treasure is still to be found.

ALEXANDER GARDEN (1730–91)
The appropriately named Garden was a part-time botanist who emigrated to South Carolina in 1752. His day job was as a doctor but it was his study of flora (and fauna) that was of longer-lasting impact. He sent samples back across the Atlantic, some to Carl Linnaeus, the founder of the natural world's taxonomy system. The *Gardenia* genus of plant was named after him by Linnaeus.

JOHN PAUL JONES (1747–92)
Jones was born near Kirkcudbright. Embarking on a naval career and arriving in America during the period of revolution against British rule, he served on ships of the Continental Navy and was successful in leading attacks on Royal Navy ships off the coast of Britain. He is regarded by the US Navy as a founding father

and in 1906 his remains were brought from France to be laid to rest in America.

JAMES GORDON BENNETT (1795–1872)
Bennett, from Keith in Aberdeenshire, emigrated in 1819. He founded the *New York Herald* newspaper and jointly founded the Associated Press. He handed control to his son, who financed Henry Stanley's expedition to find David Livingstone.

DAVID LIVINGSTONE (1813–73)
Livingstone spent much of his life in Africa. The devout Christian from Blantyre had gone as a missionary and made epic journeys across the continent. He was the first European to cast eyes on the Victoria Falls, which he named after the British monarch of the time. He later searched for the source of the River Nile.

Livingstone was hampered by illness and a left arm badly damaged in a lion attack. He was fervently against slavery and campaigned for its ending throughout his life. It had the desired effect and the main slave trading centre in East Africa was closed soon after his death.

When he was thought lost, an expedition was mounted by a New York newspaper to find him. He was famously met by Welshman Henry Stanley, who reputedly greeted him with the immortal line, 'Dr Livingstone, I presume'. When Livingstone died in 1873 his African companions carried his body to the coast – a journey that took ten months – for its onward passage to London, where he was buried in Westminster Abbey. At Ilala in Zambia, where he died, his heart was buried under a tree.

ANGUS MACASKILL (1825–63)
The 7-foot-9-inch-tall MacAskill emigrated to Canada around 1831. He is believed to be the tallest giant to have lived who was

free of medical abnormalities. His hands were a foot long and 'Giant MacAskill' was said to be so strong he could lift a horse over a fence.

ANDREW CARNEGIE (1835–1919)

Born in Dunfermline, Carnegie moved to America in 1848 where he worked at a cotton factory, a telegraph company, and a railroad company. He made wise investments in oil and heavy engineering, amongst others, but it was in iron and steel production that he was to make his name and fortune. When he sold his interest in his company in 1901, he received $447 million.

However, his accumulation of wealth was not without incident. During a strike in 1892 at Carnegie's Homestead plant, workers and private security firm Pinkerton exchanged gunfire, leaving ten men dead.

Carnegie, who was the richest man of his time, devoted much of his later life to philanthropy, including funding 2,811 free libraries with over 600 in Britain. He gave away 90 per cent of his wealth, having written in 1889: 'The man who dies thus rich, dies disgraced.'

THOMAS BLAKE GLOVER (1838–1911)

Glover was from the north-east fishing town of Fraserburgh. After having spent two years selling opium and other goods in Shanghai, in 1859, he moved to Japan.

The country was beginning to open up trading arrangements with other countries and he influenced Japan's industrialisation by importing the country's first steam locomotive, developing coal mines using Western methods and introducing modern equipment to Nagasaki's shipyard to repair ships using a steam-powered slip dock. These latter ventures later became part of Japanese company Mitsubishi. Another of Glover's entrepreneurial ventures led to the establishment of the Kirin Brewery Company.

The Scot's place in Japan's history was recognised when he became the first foreigner to be awarded the Order of the Rising Sun in 1908. It is claimed his life inspired Puccini's opera *Madama Butterfly*.

JOHN MUIR (1838-1914)

> *Only by going alone in silence, without baggage, can one truly get into the heart of the wilderness. All other travel is mere dust and hotels and baggage and chatter.*
>
> **JOHN MUIR, WRITING IN 1888**

Muir grew up in Dunbar in East Lothian. In 1849 his family emigrated to America and Muir then embarked on a series of hikes through his new homeland, which he called the 'University of the Wilderness'. He was deeply concerned with the conservation of the natural habitat and campaigned to protect Yosemite Valley in California. This resulted in it being safeguarded through its establishment as a national park in 1890. His work is credited with being a key part of establishing the environmental movement. A walking route across Scotland was named after him: The John Muir Way.

MARY SLESSOR (1848-1915)

Slessor was born in Aberdeen but moved to Dundee aged eleven, where she worked in the mills. She was inspired by the work of David Livingstone to become a missionary and in 1876 she arrived in the Calabar region of Nigeria. Slessor was appalled by the practice of abandoning or killing twins by the Efik tribespeople, who believed that in each set of twins one was naturally evil. She looked after hundreds of abandoned children and adopted nine herself. She died of malaria in 1915 and was buried in Duke Town, Calabar.

DAVID BUICK (1854–1929)
David Buick was born in Arbroath in 1854. His family emigrated two years later and settled in Detroit, Michigan. He worked for a plumbing company and developed a means of bonding enamel onto cast iron baths. In 1903 he formed the Buick Motor Company but sold his shares after losing control of the company, which went on to form part of manufacturing giant General Motors. Buick died in 1929 having lost all his money through other business ventures.

DID YOU KNOW?

The Australian city of Brisbane is named after Thomas Brisbane, a Scot from Largs, who was governor of New South Wales.

SCOTTISH PLACES ABROAD
When Scots found places in which to settle they often gave them names as a reminder of home. One example is Aberdeen, which can be found in Hong Kong, Australia (in New South Wales, Queensland and Tasmania), Canada, Jamaica, Guyana and South Africa. In the USA there are thirteen, in the states of Arkansas, California, Idaho, Kentucky, Missouri, New Jersey, Washington, Maryland, Mississippi, North Carolina, Ohio, Pennsylvania and South Dakota.

PEOPLE YOU DIDN'T KNOW WERE SCOTTISH

Defining nationality can be a tricky pursuit, but there are some well-known figures whose Scottish credentials are not in doubt.

NEIL ARMSTRONG

> *The most difficult place to be recognised is in one's own home town, and I consider this, now, my home town.*
> **NEIL ARMSTRONG, LANGHOLM, 1972**

The first person to walk on the moon in 1969 was given the freedom of the burgh of Langholm – the traditional home of the Armstrongs. The astronaut was warmly welcomed by the town and a bagpipe tune was composed for the occasion, called 'Commander Neil Armstrong's Moonstep'. In 2008 Armstrong was given an honorary degree by the University of Edinburgh, which was his first by a Scottish university.

JOHNNY CASH

The Man in Black was descended from a family in Fife, from around Falkland. Cash researched his family tree and found it went back to the twelfth century and King Malcolm IV. The move from Fife to America came when a William Cash sailed the Atlantic with the pilgrims in the 1600s. Cash's genre of country music was also linked to Scotland through Scottish folk music, which is said to have played a key part in its establishment. Cash marked his connections with his new-found heritage by playing a concert in 1981 at Falkland Palace.

AC/DC

The Australian rock band began life with three of its five members born in Scotland: singer Bon Scott was from Kirriemuir, and Angus Young (lead guitarist) and brother Malcolm (rhythm guitarist) were from Glasgow. Like many other Scots of the time, they had emigrated to start a new life in Australia in the 1950s and 1960s. In 1973 they formed what became one of rock music's biggest bands. In 2014 the Youngs' nephew Stevie joined the band, replacing Malcolm who had retired through ill health.

ELIZABETH ARDEN

Although born in Canada, Arden's father was Scottish. (Elizabeth Arden was a business name she adopted – she was born Florence Graham.) She opened a salon in New York in 1910 and built up the large beauty products business which still carries her name to this day.

DAVID BYRNE

The former Talking Heads frontman was born in Dumbarton but emigrated when two years old and grew up in Baltimore, USA.

EMMA THOMPSON

The versatile actress who appeared in *Love Actually*, *The Remains of the Day* and *Sense and Sensibility*, and who won an Oscar for her performance in *Howards End*, has a Scottish mother: Phyllida Law. Thompson's Scottish roots were used to good effect in the TV series *Tutti Frutti* where she played Glaswegian Suzi Kettles.

RELATIONS WITH ENGLAND

With a history of conflict, invasions and sporting rivalries over the centuries, it should come as no surprise that there is occasionally some tension between the two neighbouring countries. When it was announced in 1707 that there was to be a union between Scotland and England, there was widespread disorder in the streets of Edinburgh. Three hundred years later, when tennis player Andy Murray said he would support 'anyone but England' in a football tournament, he received much criticism from those who didn't appreciate the Scotsman's dry humour.

With so much cross-border interaction nowadays, the English are not seen as the 'Auld Enemy' of the past and for many Scots the country south of the border is a place that can even be lived in. A 2009 Scottish government study found that of the 5.5 million people who were born in Scotland almost 800,000 lived in England.

DID YOU KNOW?

John Bull was created by a Scotsman. This personification of England was written by Inverbervie's John Arbuthnot in the eighteenth century.

DID YOU KNOW?

The word *sassenach* (from the Gaelic 'sasunnach') means a Saxon, an English person or an English-speaking person from the Scottish lowlands.

HISTORY

Humans had lived in Scotland for thousands of years but it wasn't until the arrival of the Romans that history began to be written down, which serves as a good starting point for Scotland's recorded history.

TIMELINE

AD 83   The Romans defeat Calgacus's Caledonians at the Battle of Mons Graupius.

122   Construction begins on Hadrian's Wall.

142   Construction begins on the Antonine Wall.

208   Emperor Septimius Severus leads last Roman attempt to conquer Scotland.

397   Saint Ninian establishes first Christian church in Scotland at Whithorn.

410   Romans leave Britain.

563   Saint Columba establishes monastery on Iona, ushering in a new era of religious worship in Scotland.

685   Bridei's Picts defeat the Angles of King Ecgfrith of Northumbria at the Battle of Nechtansmere (Dun Nechtain).

847   King Kenneth MacAlpin becomes the first to rule over Scots and Picts.

1040   Macbeth becomes king.

1072   Treaty of Abernethy gives Malcolm III lands in Cumbria in return for swearing allegiance to Norman king William the Conqueror.

1124   David I becomes king.

1174   Treaty of Falaise gives rights of supremacy over Scotland to English king Henry II.

1263   Norwegians are defeated at the Battle of Largs and the Hebrides become part of Scotland.

1286   King Alexander III dies and the lack of a suitable heir leads to years of conflict.

1291   Edward I oversees the appointment of John Balliol as Scottish king.

1295   The Auld Alliance is formed with France.

1296   John Balliol is deposed after militarily opposing Edward I.

1297   William Wallace scores a major victory over English forces at the Battle of Stirling Bridge.

1298   Edward I defeats William Wallace at the Battle of Falkirk.

1305   William Wallace is captured and executed in London.

1306   Robert the Bruce is crowned King of Scotland.

1314   Robert the Bruce wins a famous victory at the Battle of Bannockburn.

1320   Declaration of Arbroath declares Scottish sovereignty.

1371   Robert II becomes the first Stewart king.

1413   Scotland's first university is founded at St Andrews.

1469   Orkney and Shetland become part of Scotland.

1513   King James IV and thousands of others die at the Battle of Flodden.

1542   At the Battle of Solway Moss, the Scottish army suffers a heavy defeat by a numerically smaller English army.

1544   The Rough Wooing, Henry VIII's military campaign to secure a marriage between his son Edward and Scots princess Mary, begins.

1546   George Wishart is burned; Cardinal Beaton is murdered by Protestants.

1560 Treaty of Edinburgh sees all French and English troops leave Scotland.

1560 Reformation takes place, installing Protestantism as the established religion of Scotland.

1561 Mary, Queen of Scots, returns to Scotland.

1567 Mary, Queen of Scots, abdicates.

1587 Mary, Queen of Scots, is executed.

1603 Union of the Crowns takes place as King James VI accedes to the English throne, following the death of Elizabeth I.

1637 Jenny Geddes leads protests in Edinburgh's St Giles' Cathedral over imposition by James VI of a revised prayer book for Scotland.

1638 Resistance to Charles I's imposition of religious control is formalised by the signing of the National Covenant at Edinburgh's Greyfriars Kirk.

1643 Solemn League and Covenant is signed which allies the Scottish Covenanters with the English Parliament against Charles I.

1649 Charles I is executed.

1651 Charles II is crowned King of Scotland.

1660 Restoration of Charles II.

1689   The Jacobites defeat government forces but lose their
        commander Viscount 'Bonnie' Dundee at the Battle
        of Killiecrankie.

1692   In the Massacre of Glencoe, members of the
        MacDonald clan are murdered by government troops.

1698   The Darien expedition begins as Scotland attempts to
        create its own colony in Central America.

1707   The Act of Union unites the parliaments of Scotland
        and England.

1715   At the Battle of Sheriffmuir, Jacobite forces fail to
        take advantage of superior numbers against
        Hanoverian troops.

1745   Jacobite uprising begins, led by Bonnie Prince Charlie
        as he attempts to regain the crown for the Stewarts.

1746   The Jacobites are defeated by government troops at the
        Battle of Culloden, the last major battle on British soil.

1776   Adam Smith's *The Wealth of Nations* is published.

1786   Robert Burns' *Poems, Chiefly in the Scottish Dialect*
        is published.

1814   Walter Scott's *Waverley* is published.

1843   Disruption of the kirk sees a schism develop in the
        Church of Scotland and the Free Church of Scotland
        is created.

1879   Tay Rail Bridge collapses, killing seventy-five people.

1890   Forth Bridge is completed.

1901   The Glasgow International Exhibition sees the opening of a Glasgow landmark: the new Art Gallery and Museum in Kelvingrove Park.

1914   First World War begins.

1919   Red Clydeside protest sees mass rally in Glasgow's George Square.

1924   Ramsay MacDonald becomes first Labour prime minister.

1934   Scottish National Party formed.

1938   Empire Exhibition opens at Bellahouston Park, Glasgow. Over six months it will receive over twelve million visitors.

1939   Second World War begins.

1941   Clydebank heavily bombed.

1945   Robert McIntyre becomes the SNP's first Westminster MP.

1947   The first Edinburgh Festival is held.

1971   Sixty-six Rangers football fans are killed in the Ibrox disaster.

1975   North Sea oil production begins.

1979   Scots voters reject devolution in a referendum.

1982   Pope John Paul II makes first-ever visit to Scotland
        as pontiff.

1988   Piper Alpha disaster results in deaths of 167 North Sea
        oil workers.

1988   A Pan Am Boeing 747 explodes over Lockerbie,
        killing 270.

1999   Scottish Parliament reconvenes.

2009   Lockerbie bomber Abdul Baset al-Megrahi is released
        from a Scottish jail.

2013   Andy Murray wins Wimbledon for the first time.

2014   Independence referendum is a defeat for the 'Yes'
        campaign advocating that Scotland becomes an
        independent country.

FROM EARLY TIMES TO WARS OF INDEPENDENCE

EARLY HUMANS IN SCOTLAND

Since the end of the last ice age, about 10,000 years ago, humans started to appear on the land that would become Scotland. These early peoples were hunter-gatherers. The period of around 10000 BC to 5000 BC is known as the Mesolithic era and it gave way to the Neolithic era (around 4000 BC to 2000 BC). These early Scots started to build houses and make tools from stone. They also started to farm, and hunted and fished for food. Some of their habitats have survived, including at Skara Brae in Orkney and Jarlshof in Shetland. They used bronze and later iron for weapons, jewellery and tools – and these materials were the names retrospectively given to the periods of time up until the middle of the first millennium AD. The Scots in the early part of the first millennium AD were organised into hierarchical social structures. They built brochs (defensive towers) on land and crannogs (buildings on stilts) in the lochs.

DID YOU KNOW?

The Orkney Venus has nothing to do with astronomy, but is the name given to a small stone Neolithic carving of a woman found on the island of Westray in Orkney in 2009. Also given the name Westray Wife, she is believed to be the earliest representation of the human figure found in Scotland, dating back 5,000 years.

THE ROMANS IN SCOTLAND

The Romans arrived in Scotland in the first century AD, signalling the end of the prehistoric eras. They made three major attempts to conquer Scotland (which they called Caledonia). Julius Agricola led the first invasion, resulting in the victorious Battle of Mons Graupius, in the north-east of Scotland in AD 83. The leader of the Caledonians was Calgacus – the first Scot to be individually identified in history. However, a few years later the Romans withdrew south of the Forth as troop numbers were redeployed to other areas of the Roman Empire. By the end of the first century, they had withdrawn to the Solway–Tyne line.

In 122, the huge defensive structure of Hadrian's Wall, running from the Solway to the Tyne, was begun, but this was superseded in the early 140s as a more northerly defensive line between the Forth and Clyde was established, called the Antonine Wall, after Emperor Antoninus Pius.

However, in the 160s, the Antonine Wall was abandoned in the face of resistance and the Romans fell back to Hadrian's Wall. The wall came under attack and by the end of the second century the northern tribes had broken through, eventually reaching York.

These northern tribes were pushed back and in 208 Emperor Septimius Severus carried out a large-scale offensive on the Caledonians, in the north-east of Scotland, and the Maeatae, located north of the Forth–Clyde isthmus. He reached the Moray Firth but his successes were undone when he died in 211 and his son Caracalla abandoned the offensive.

Hadrian's Wall had been restored as the northernmost part of the Roman Empire and remained in place for almost a century. There were other offensives, such as in 305–6 by Constantius Chlorus, but the Romans had given up their aim of completing the Roman conquest of Britain.

In 367 the wall was breached by Picts. The Romans also came under pressure on the west coast of England and Wales from invaders from Ireland. Saxons invaded the south-east in what appeared to be a coordinated offensive – given the name the Barbarian Conspiracy. The Romans restored their position but within decades they were no longer in power in Britain, having never succeeded in conquering Scotland.

Hadrian's Wall

It begins in the west at Bowness-on-Solway and runs 73 miles to the appropriately named Wallsend on the River Tyne. Taking six years to complete, the stone wall was 15 feet high and 8 feet thick. Forts called milecastles were incorporated along its length every Roman mile. Despite the stones being used for local building, sections still remain.

Antonine Wall

Its construction, which began in AD 142, differed from Hadrian's Wall in that it was made of turf on top of stone, with a deep ditch in front. It was 10 feet high and 14 feet thick. Running 37 miles, from Old Kilpatrick in the west to Bo'ness in the east, the wall was guarded by seventeen forts. In the 160s, the wall was abandoned. Parts of it disappeared as the land was developed during the Industrial Revolution but sections remain.

Caledonians and Maeatae

Roman historian Cassius Dio wrote many books on Roman history. In volume LXXVII (seventy-seven) he describes the Caledonians and the Maeatae:

> *The Maeatae live next to the cross-wall which cuts the island in half, and the Caledonians are beyond them. They dwell in tents, naked and unshod, possess their women in common, and in common rear all the offspring. Their form of rule is democratic for the most part, and they are very fond of plundering; consequently, they choose their boldest men as rulers. They go into battle in chariots, and have small, swift horses; there are also foot-soldiers, very swift in running and very firm in standing their ground.*

The Cramond Lioness

In 1996 a ferryman at Cramond in Edinburgh spotted something unusual in the mud. When the object was retrieved it was found to be a 5-foot-long Roman stone sculpture depicting a lioness attacking a bearded man. Cramond had been the site of a Roman fort and the lioness was thought to be a memorial to a senior officer.

ANGLES, BRITONS, PICTS, SCOTS AND VIKINGS

By the end of the ninth century there were five peoples living in Scotland:

Angles

Area: From the Firth of Forth southwards (also in England down to the River Humber).

The Germanic Angles had advanced northwards to establish territory in Scotland. Their ambitions to gain more land were halted in 685 by the Picts at Nechtansmere in Angus.

Britons

Area: Strathclyde.

Following the departure of the Romans, the Britons in Britain had lost territory to the Angles and Saxons, and in Scotland became centred around Dumbarton. In 870 a siege by the Vikings destroyed their headquarters and further weakened their position.

Picts

Area: From the Forth to the most northerly parts of Scotland.

The Picts were so-called by the Romans as the name means 'the painted people'. Little is known about these occupiers of northern Scotland as no written records have survived, although standing stones featuring depictions of warriors still exist.

Scots (Gaels)

Area: Argyll (Dál Riata).

From Ireland, the Scots (the Romans called them the Scotti) had settled in the west, in what we know as Argyll, but became known as Dál Riata. Kenneth MacAlpin, who was King of the Scots, also became leader of the Picts in 843.

Vikings

These seafaring Scandinavians were able to gain territory in Scotland at the expense of the other tribes, in the north and west, namely Shetland, Orkney, parts of Argyll, the northern Highlands and the Outer Hebrides.

GREAT SCOT
SAINT COLUMBA (521-97)

Columba was not the only missionary to attempt to convert the early inhabitants of Scotland to Christianity, but he is the most known. Despite being one of the great figures in Scottish history, he was not born a Scot. Also called Colum Cille (Church Dove), he was born in 521 in Ireland's County Donegal. Raised as a member of an Irish royal family, he was ordained and spent fifteen years in Ireland preaching and establishing monasteries before he travelled to Scotland and, in 563, established a monastery on the Hebridean island of Iona. It is claimed that Columba was forced into exile as penance for causing a battle that led to a large loss of lives.

In Scotland, he preached to the pagan Picts and it has been claimed he converted the Pictish king Bridei. Columba died in 597 having established Iona as a major centre of the Christian religion, which would eventually be adopted across the whole country.

DID YOU KNOW?

A relic of Saint Columba was reputedly carried at the Battle of Bannockburn in 1314. The relic was believed to have been placed in a small wooden, silver and bronze object – called the Monymusk Reliquary – which can be seen in the National Museum of Scotland in Edinburgh.

DID YOU KNOW?

The Book of Kells was created in Scotland. The beautifully illustrated book of the Gospels is thought to have been produced on Iona around 800, before being taken to Ireland in the face of Viking attacks. It is now on display in Trinity College, Dublin.

DUNADD

Dunadd in Argyll and Bute was the centre of the Scots' kingdom of Dál Riata for three centuries. A fort occupied the rocky outcrop and one unusual feature is a footprint, carved out of the rock. It is said that a man about to become king would place his foot in the hole to cement his relationship with the land. With King Kenneth MacAlpin taking over Pictland in the ninth century, Dunadd ceased to be the royal home.

DID YOU KNOW?

Reflecting its importance in early Scottish history, there are over 350 ancient sites within a few miles of Dunadd, some dating back to Neolithic times.

MACBETH

Macbeth became King of Scots in 1040 after he killed King Duncan I in battle. Macbeth was challenged by Duncan's son Malcolm Canmore at Dunsinane in 1054, and then later in 1057 at Lumphanan where Macbeth died. Despite his portrayal by Shakespeare, he was a just ruler who oversaw a kingdom tranquil enough to allow him to make a pilgrimage to Rome – the only Scottish monarch to do so.

GREAT SCOT
SAINT MARGARET (c.1045–93)

I may say every word which she uttered, every act which she performed, showed that she was meditating upon the things of heaven.
TURGOT, BISHOP OF ST ANDREWS, THE LIFE OF ST MARGARET, QUEEN OF SCOTLAND

Born in Hungary around 1045, Margaret moved to England then Scotland following the Norman invasion of 1066. She wished to enter a nunnery but instead married King Malcolm III. The success of a royal marriage depended on the production of heirs, and Malcolm and Margaret's can therefore be ranked highly: they had eight children, all of whom lived to adulthood. Three of their six sons became kings and Matilda, the eldest daughter, became Queen of England when she married Henry I.

Margaret devoted her life to religious observance and charitable deeds although she fasted so much it affected her health. She provided shelter for pilgrims travelling to St Andrews, thus giving rise to the villages on the Forth of North and South Queensferry. She helped and fed the poor each day. Canonised in 1250, she is remembered through the many statues, buildings, streets and organisations named after her, which include:

☒ Queen Margaret University (Edinburgh)

☒ Queen Margaret College (Glasgow)

☒ Queen Margaret Drive (Glasgow)

☒ Queen Margaret Union (students' union, Glasgow)

☒ Queen Margaret Hospital (Dunfermline)

☒ St Margaret of Scotland Hospice (Clydebank)

☒ St Margaret's Academy (Livingston)

☒ St Margaret's High School (Airdrie)

☒ St Margaret's School for Girls (Aberdeen)

☒ St Margaret's School (York)

FAMILY TIES

In 1072, William the Conqueror invaded Scotland, in response to a raid on England by King Malcolm III. William met Malcolm at Abernethy in Perthshire and peace was made. In return, Malcolm submitted to the Norman king and Malcolm's eldest son, Duncan, was taken south as hostage. He was brought up as part of the English court.

On Malcolm's death in 1094, Duncan returned to Scotland to take the crown, which had been given to his uncle Donald Bane. Duncan was successful and Donald was defeated, however, Duncan had been supported by English and French troops and their presence in Scotland was resented so Duncan was forced to send them south. This left him weak: when Donald returned, Duncan was killed. He had reigned for less than year.

FEUDALISM

David I became King of Scotland in 1124. Having grown up in the English court, he was familiar with feudal ways and encouraged Norman nobles to settle in Scotland to help bring feudalism to the country. One of these noblemen was Robert de Brus from the Cherbourg area, who was given land in Annandale. Castles built on the Norman motte design were to be seats of power in the new sheriffdoms. David was also active in expanding and organising the Church: the four Border Abbeys were founded in his reign. He set up burghs and by the end of his rule, in 1153, Scotland had many of the medieval elements of society established.

THE GREAT CAUSE

When King Alexander III died in 1286 his granddaughter, the three-year-old Maid of Norway, was next in line for the throne. In 1290, on her way to become queen, she died in Orkney. English King Edward I adjudicated on who was to be the next king, known as the Great Cause, and eventually chose John

Balliol. His rule did not guarantee stability as he had accepted the overlordship of Edward and not all in Scotland agreed with this. Noblemen rejected Edward's rule and in 1296 the English king invaded Scotland, which led to Balliol being removed from the throne.

NICKNAMES OF EARLY SCOTS KINGS

'Auld Bleary'	Robert II (1316–90)
'Big Head'	Malcolm III (1031–93)
'The Fierce'	Alexander I (*c.*1078–1124)
'The Madman'	Donald II (*c.*860–900)
'The Foolish'	Lulach (*c.*1030–58)
'The Diseased'	Duncan I (*c.*1001–40)
'The Fair'	Donald III (*c.*1040–99)
'The Maiden'	Malcolm IV (1141–65)
'The Lion'	William I (1143–1214)
'The Destroyer'	Malcolm II (*c.*954–1034)
'Toom Tabard' (Empty Coat)	John Balliol (1249–1314)

GREAT SCOT
WILLIAM WALLACE (DIED 1305)

William Wallace is a man of whom little is known but of whom much has been said. There are few certain facts: there is even uncertainty over where he was born, with competing claims between Elderslie near Paisley and Ellerslie in Ayrshire.

In 1297, as unrest against the English rule of Scotland under Edward I spread, Wallace killed the English sheriff of Lanark, William Heselrig. Support for Wallace grew and he traversed Scotland attacking the occupying forces. With Andrew Murray, who had led the uprising in the north of the country, Wallace faced an English army at Stirling Bridge on 11 September 1297. Before the battle, the English had sent Dominican friars to mediate for a peaceful settlement. Wallace is reported to have replied:

> *Tell your people that we have not come here for*
> *peace: we are ready to fight to avenge ourselves*
> *and to free our country. Let them come up to us as*
> *soon as they like, and they will find us prepared*
> *to prove the same in their beards.*

The ensuing battle was a great success for the Scots, with their opponents losing as many as 5,000 dead. Among them was the English treasurer Hugh de Cressingham – it was claimed Wallace had a belt made from his skin.

Wallace led raids into England, and Edward I, who had returned from the Continent, took his forces into Scotland. Now knighted and made Guardian of Scotland, Wallace was forced to face Edward's army in a pitched battle at Falkirk on 22 July 1298. Chances of victory were hindered by the cavalry of the Scots nobles leaving the field. The Scots army was heavily defeated.

Wallace spent time in France but returned to Scotland to continue the armed struggle, yet he was regarded as an outlaw and Edward offered rewards to those who could secure his capture. In August 1305, he was captured and taken to London, where he was quickly tried and found guilty. His punishment was outlined thus:

> *He should be hanged and afterwards drawn. And*
> *because he had been outlawed and not afterwards*
> *restored to the King's peace, he should be*
> *beheaded and decapitated. And also because he*
> *had committed both murders and felonies, not only*
> *to the lord the King himself but to the entire people*
> *of England and Scotland, the body of that William*
> *should be cut up and divided and cut up into four*

> *quarters, and that the head thus cut off should be affixed upon London bridge in the sight of those crossing both by land and by water, and one quarter should be hung on the gibbet at Newcastle upon Tyne, another quarter at Berwick, a third quarter at Stirling, and a fourth quarter at St John's town [Perth] as a cause of fear and chastisement of all going past and looking upon these things.*

This wasn't the end of his punishment. Wallace's heart, liver and lungs were burned for his 'measureless wickedness' to the Church.

MONUMENTS
Ballarat, Australia (statue)
Baltimore, USA (statue)
Barnweil, Ayrshire
Dryburgh (statue)
Edinburgh Castle (statue)
Lanark (statue)
Robroyston (memorial cross)
The National Wallace Monument, Abbey Craig, Stirling
Wallace Cairn, South Ayrshire
Wallace Tower, South Ayrshire
Wallacestone Monument, Falkirk

THE DOUGLAS LARDER
This was the name given to a gruesome event of 1307 in the Wars of Independence whereby English soldiers were captured and beheaded by men under the 'Good' Sir James Douglas. Their heads were put on top of food stores and then set alight.

GREAT SCOT
ROBERT THE BRUCE (1274-1329)

Without Robert the Bruce, it is possible that Scotland would not have the national identity it does to this day. He was able to resist English dominance and establish his own kingship from the gravest of beginnings.

His grandfather 'The Competitor' had aspirations to become king but was unsuccessful when Edward I gave the crown to John Balliol in 1292. Robert, who had spent time in King Edward I's court, initially did not appear to have great ambitions to be the King of Scotland. He was on Edward's side in 1296 when war broke out, but in 1297 Bruce turned against Edward I and the English occupation. He took the side of the deposed King John Balliol, but surrendered months later.

In 1298, after William Wallace resigned the guardianship of Scotland he had held in the absence of a monarch, Robert the Bruce was made joint guardian with John Comyn, of a rival family, but Comyn was able to have Bruce removed by 1300.

Bruce again sided with Edward I in 1302, and helped in the hunt for William Wallace, but this was not to remain his position. In a dramatic moment in February 1306, Bruce killed John Comyn in Greyfriars Kirk in Dumfries. This heinous crime – even in the brutal and bloody medieval era – saw Bruce excommunicated. It also saw him become king, as he rode to Scone where he had himself crowned in March.

There was no auspicious start to his reign and he was forced into exile but, like the mythical spider (see page 220), he did not give up. He was helped by the death of Edward I in 1307, as the new English king Edward II was not as militarily adept as his father. Bruce successfully attacked his rivals in Scotland and by 1309 held his first parliament. He kept his hold on his kingdom and, in 1314, won the great Battle of Bannockburn. It didn't secure Scotland's independence, which would take a further fourteen years before England finally accepted the sovereignty of Bruce's Scotland, but his excommunication was rescinded before he died in 1329.

BRUCE'S AXE

The main battle of Bannockburn was fought on 24 June 1314, but the evening prior to this there were several skirmishes. One particular incident involved only two people and was to enter legend. An English knight named Henry de Bohun spotted the Scottish king and quickly charged towards him, lance in position. Bruce was unarmoured and riding a small pony. At the last minute, he moved away from the charging knight, rose up in his stirrups and, employing the only weapon he had, brought an axe down onto de Bohun's head, cleaving both his helmet and skull in twain. He casually remarked that it was a pity, as he thought it a good axe. Bruce was reproached by his noblemen for risking it all for this one-to-one combat, but the quick-thinking king's victory was a boost to his army's morale.

DECLARATION OF ARBROATH

For, as long as a hundred of us remain alive,
never will we on any conditions be subjected
to the lordship of the English. It is in truth not
for glory, nor riches, nor honours that we are
fighting, but for freedom alone, which no honest
man gives up but with life itself.
DECLARATION OF ARBROATH, 1320

The Declaration of 1320 was actually a letter to the Pope, requesting his assistance in asking England to let Scotland live in peace. It contained perhaps the most famous passage in Scottish history – a declaration of the nation's independence from England.

POST-BRUCE

The period after Robert the Bruce's death in 1329 was not one of tranquillity. The 1328 Treaty of Edinburgh–Northampton was supposed to ensure peace between England and Scotland but war broke out again and the English won a large victory at Halidon Hill in 1333, which was seen as revenge for Bannockburn. The Scottish economy suffered as a result of having to pay a literal king's ransom of 100,000 merks to secure the release of King David II when he was taken prisoner and kept in the Tower of London for eleven years following the Battle of Neville's Cross.

In 1371 he was succeeded by Robert II, the first king of a family that was to dominate Scottish history for several centuries: the Stewarts. Robert II was Robert the Bruce's grandson but possessed none of that king's skills or character. He acceded to the throne, aged fifty-five, and was a weak ruler. His son succeeded him but he was also not a strong character. When his son James was captured by English pirates, Robert III died shortly after from a broken heart. He left behind his own epitaph:

Here lies the worst of kings and most wretched
of men in the whole kingdom.

RENAISSANCE TO THE JACOBITE REBELLION

THE FIFTEENTH CENTURY

The fifteenth century saw more strife, much of it domestic, as a succession of minority monarchs were unable to quell the power of strong noblemen. The Stewart kings James I, II, III and IV battled with families such as the powerful Douglases. James III also faced challenges from his son and brothers.

THE FIRST JAMESES

JAMES I

Reign: 1406–37

Age at succession: 11

Details of reign: Was captured on his way to France (where he was being sent for safekeeping) and held captive in England for eighteen years. Faced resistance to his rule in the Highlands as well as from nobles.

Fate: He was stabbed by nobles, who were unhappy at his taxation policies, after hiding in a sewer.

JAMES II

Reign: 1437–60

Age at succession: 6

Details of reign: Took over governing the country aged eighteen. Fought the Douglas family and, in 1452, stabbed the Earl of Douglas to death in Stirling Castle. Was besieging the English-held Roxburgh Castle when he died.

Fate: Killed by an exploding cannon.

JAMES III

Reign: 1460–88

Age at succession: 8

Details of reign: James tried to maintain peace with England but in 1482 English forces made their way to Scotland to support James's brother, the Duke of Albany, and James was imprisoned. He regained power and in 1488 faced his troublesome nobles at Sauchieburn, where he was defeated. His son James was on the rebels' side.

Fate: After being thrown from a horse at the Battle of Sauchieburn, he was stabbed to death by a passer-by.

THE BLACK DINNER

One of the most infamous tales of Edinburgh Castle is that of the Black Dinner. The story goes that the keeper of the castle invited the sixteen-year-old sixth Earl of Douglas and his brother to dinner on 24 November 1440. After they had eaten, a bull's head, which is a symbol of death, was presented in front of the two guests. The two were summarily tried for treason and beheaded against the protests of ten-year-old King James II. This assassination was to quell the power of the Douglas nobles.

DID YOU KNOW?

The Black Dinner served as inspiration for an event in George R. R. Martin's *Game of Thrones*.

GARDE ÉCOSSAISE

Scottish soldiers fought alongside Joan of Arc during the Hundred Years War and, as the Garde Écossaise, King Louis XI employed them for personal protection.

DID YOU KNOW?

During the fifteenth century, three universities were founded in Scotland:

1413   St Andrews
1451   Glasgow
1495   Aberdeen (King's College)

Edinburgh followed a century later in 1582. The universities were established to train clerics.

GREAT SCOT
KING JAMES IV (1473–1513)

*He had a wonderful force of intellect, an
incredible knowledge of all things.*
ERASMUS ON JAMES IV

In 1488, James IV succeeded to the throne, aged fifteen. He was a popular king, religiously devout and courageous. In the Renaissance era, he supported the arts and during his reign the first printing press in Scotland was established. He oversaw a period of prosperity as Scotland's burghs traded with Europe. James made attempts at improving relations with clan chiefs in the Highlands, although these weren't wholly successful. Relations with Scotland's southern neighbour were always crucial to the well-being of the country and its monarchs, so James made moves to secure the peace: in 1502 Scotland signed a treaty of Perpetual Peace with England and the next year he married Margaret Tudor, the daughter of English king Henry VII. However, peace was not to 'endure forever', as the treaty had stated; in 1512 James renewed Scotland's support for its Auld Alliance partner when England, along with other European powers, moved against France. In 1513, James led a large Scottish army into England. At Flodden on 9 September his army suffered a heavy defeat that saw as many as 10,000 Scots die. James himself was killed. A Scots lament called 'The Flowers o' the Forest' was written about those who died.

GREAT MICHAEL

James IV was keen to have Scotland play an important role in foreign affairs and he embarked on a programme of building a powerful fleet of warships. The largest of these was the *Great Michael* which was built in Newhaven and launched in 1511. It was said that all the trees in Fife were used in its construction. At

240 feet long, it was the biggest warship in Europe – twice the size of the *Mary Rose*. The ship was hugely expensive to build and run, and eventually it was sold to France at a much-reduced price.

NOBLE NICKNAMES

'The Grim'	Archibald Douglas, third Earl of Douglas (*c*.1328–1400)
'The Gross'	James Douglas, seventh Earl of Douglas (1371–1443)
'Black Douglas'/'The Good Sir James'	Sir James Douglas (*c*.1286–1330)
'The Bastard of Arran'	Sir James Hamilton of Finnart (*c*.1495–1540)
'The Flower of Chivalry'/'The Knight of Liddesdale'	Sir William Douglas (*c*.1300–53)
'William of the Tower'	William Keith, fourth Earl Marischal (1506–81)
'Longleg'	William, Lord of Douglas (*c*.1220–*c*.1274)
'The Bold'	Sir William Douglas (*c*.1240–98)
'The Dull'	Hugh, Lord of Douglas (1294–*c*.1346)
'Bell the Cat'	Archibald Douglas, fifth Earl of Angus (1453–1513)

THE REFORMATION

In the sixteenth century, Protestants in Europe attempted to change the way religious worship and governance was carried out, creating discontent. The questioning of the Church began when German theologian Martin Luther published his Theses in 1517, which criticised the selling of indulgences, i.e. a way of buying remission from sin. The Frenchman John Calvin taught many pastors this new way of religious thinking at the College of Geneva. In England, in 1534, King Henry VIII abandoned Catholicism for Protestantism in order to secure a male heir.

The Catholic Church in Scotland was wealthy and able to provide for the immoral (as seen by those seeking reform) behaviour of its bishops and other religious figures. Those benefitting from its largesse faced a popular movement of dissenters. One of these was Patrick Hamilton, who was burnt at the stake in St Andrews on the orders of Archbishop James Beaton. Beaton's nephew David replaced his uncle as archbishop at St Andrews and became a cardinal. He was allied with the French Catholic Queen Mother, Mary of Guise, with whom he attempted to thwart the reformers, whose cause was spreading through the country.

Another dissenter was George Wishart, and he was also burnt to death in St Andrews. The reformers were not averse to using violence and in 1546 they murdered Cardinal Beaton, stabbing and throwing him out the window of his residence. His last words were reputed to be 'All is gone'. French forces captured the bishop's assassins and one of the men implicated was John Knox, a chaplain in St Andrews. He was sent as a prisoner to the French galleys where he remained until 1549. Knox spent time with John Calvin in Geneva and when he returned to Scotland in 1559 the Protestant cause had a powerful and vocal figurehead. Churches were attacked and statues were smashed by mobs.

As always, matters south of the border were to play an important part in Scotland's history. In 1558 Elizabeth succeeded to the throne of England. She was Protestant and replaced the Catholic Mary Tudor. The Scottish Protestants felt support would come from England and in 1560 English ships brought troops to face those French troops sent to support Mary of Guise, who was now Regent of Scotland. When Mary died that same year, the subsequent Treaty of Edinburgh resulted in the removal of French and English troops from Scotland. With the Catholic Regent gone, the way was clear for the reformers to install their new Church. It would lead to a more austere environment, with an end to celebrating Christmas and Easter and with churches devoid of decoration. Mass carried out in Latin was forbidden.

> *To promote a woman to bear rule,*
> *superiority, dominion, or empire above*
> *any realm, nation, or city, is repugnant to*
> *nature; contumely to God, a thing most*
> *contrary to his revealed will and approved*
> *ordinance; and finally, it is the subversion*
> *of good order, of all equity and justice.*
>
> **JOHN KNOX, THE FIRST BLAST OF THE TRUMPET AGAINST**
> **THE MONSTROUS REGIMENT* OF WOMEN (1558)**

Knox wrote his pamphlet in Geneva while exiled from Catholic Britain. He was in outspoken opposition to the rule of Catholic women: Mary Tudor in England, and Mary of Guise and her daughter Mary in Scotland. Knox's attack on women's ability to rule backfired when Elizabeth I acceded to the English throne in

---

* The phrase 'monstrous regiment' has an old meaning, which translates to 'unnatural rule'.

1558. Although his words were not aimed at her, she did not take kindly to the sentiment and barred him from entry to England.

GREAT SCOT
MARY, QUEEN OF SCOTS (1542–87)

One of Scottish history's most well-known figures, Mary Stuart (she adopted the French spelling of her surname) succeeded to the throne aged less than one week old in 1542. Born to a French mother, Mary of Guise, she was moved to France in 1548 after English king Henry VIII – who had designs on Scotland and wished Mary to marry his son Edward – began a violent campaign known as the Rough Wooing. In 1558 she married the Dauphin in Notre Dame Cathedral but it was not to last – he died two years later.

Mary returned to a turbulent Scotland. Protestantism was the established religion but she was a Catholic queen and her subjects' loyalties to their monarch came up against the feelings against her religion. John Knox was a fierce enemy of the queen, who wished to continue to practise her religion, but without wishing to impose it on her subjects.

In 1565 Mary married her cousin Henry, Lord Darnley. He was not to prove a capable partner in life and his distrust of the queen's assistant, David Rizzio, led to the Italian being murdered in front of the pregnant Mary. A year later it was Darnley who was dead, following an explosion at Kirk o' Field in Edinburgh.

One of the Scottish nobles, James Hepburn, the Earl of Bothwell, was thought to be involved in the plot to kill Darnley. Within a couple of months of Darnley's death, Mary married Hepburn. Her decision to marry him was ill-thought-out, although there are theories she was forced to marry him after being raped. Whatever the reasons, matters were now in train that would lead to her downfall. Protestant nobles defeated the queen's forces at Carberry Hill and she was led through the streets of Edinburgh. She was held captive on Loch Leven and abdicated her crown. Mary escaped to England, where she hoped her cousin, the Queen of England, would protect her. Fearing the presence of a rival to her own crown, Elizabeth kept her captive. In 1586 Mary was convicted of plotting to assassinate Elizabeth and the following year, after nineteen years of captivity, was executed for treason. She said to the executioner, 'I hope you shall make an end of all my troubles.'

THE UNION OF THE CROWNS

It is impossible that Scottis men and Inglis men
can remain in concord under ane monarchy
or ane prince because their naturis and
conditiouns are as indefferent as is the nature
of sheep and wolves.

ROBERT WEDDERBURN,
THE COMPLAYNT OF SCOTLAND (1549)

On 24 March 1603, Queen Elizabeth died with no children of her own. The next monarch was north of the border: James VI of Scotland – Mary, Queen of Scots' own son. James had been raised as a Protestant and, despite centuries of feuding between the two countries, that was all that mattered. This was the first time a Scot was to sit on the throne in England.

James wasted little time in heading south and was crowned James I of England at Westminster Abbey that July. He was not hugely popular with the English court, as he was perceived to be favouring the Scots, but his uniting of the crowns of two countries that had long waged war was his legacy. When he died in 1625 he was succeeded by his son Charles I. James returned to Scotland only once in his reign.

WITCH-HUNTS

Among the darkest practices in Scottish history were witch-hunts: the persecution of thousands of women and men on charges of witchcraft. It is thought that up to 4,000 people, mostly women, were prosecuted with up to two-thirds being executed, from the middle of the sixteenth century to the start of the eighteenth century. King James VI instigated a campaign against witchcraft after he believed they had conspired to raise a storm while he was at sea. He wrote a book in 1597 called *Daemonologie* on the subject.

THE COVENANTERS AND CIVIL WAR

We promise and swear by the great name of the Lord our God, to continue in the profession and obedience of the aforesaid religion; that we shall defend the same, and resist all these contrary errors and corruptions according to our vocation, and to the utmost of that power that God hath put into our hands, all the days of our life.
THE NATIONAL COVENANT, 1638

The National Covenant served as the opposition to King Charles I's religious instructions on the Scottish people, in particular to the king's appointment of bishops. The ensuing conflict began in 1639 with the first Bishops' War and led to the English Civil War of 1642. Scots fought on Oliver Cromwell's victorious side at Marston Moor but in Scotland itself James Graham, the fifth Earl of Montrose, fought on the king's side against the Covenanters. Charles I surrendered to Scottish troops at Newark in 1646, but when he refused to install Presbyterianism in England the Scots handed him over to Cromwell and he was subsequently executed in 1649.

Conflict was not over. Scotland proclaimed Charles I's son as king and this provoked Cromwell into invasion. He went on to secure control over the whole country and Charles II fled to Europe. In 1660, following Cromwell's death, Charles returned to take his place on the throne again. He oversaw reverses in the arrangements governing the Church north of the border: bishops were reintroduced and ministers were to be appointed by these bishops. While most church ministers accepted the changes, some chose to reject this interference and these 'outed ministers' held services away from their churches in conventicles. The government sought to suppress this unauthorised worship through torture and the imposition of the death penalty for those preaching.

Armed rebellion took place and in 1679 the Archbishop of St Andrews was assassinated. The Covenanters won the battle at Drumclog but lost at Bothwell Brig. Twelve hundred Covenanters were forced into Greyfriars Kirkyard in Edinburgh where they were kept until they were executed, died from disease, escaped or accepted terms to enter 'the king's peace'. Around two hundred of those who refused to sign a pledge to the monarch were transported to the West Indies but died when their ship sank near Orkney. Given the job of enforcing the government's orders was John Graham, Laird of Claverhouse, who was given the name Bluidy Clavers as a result. This period became known as the Killing Time.

THE 1689 JACOBITE UPRISING

In 1688, James VI's son, James VII and II, was deposed from the British throne, as a result of his religion (he was Catholic), and replaced by Protestant Dutchman Prince William of Orange, who was married to James's daughter Mary. James's supporters were called Jacobites, after the Latin word for James: *Jacobus*. In Scotland, troops loyal to King James were commanded by

Bluidy Clavers, who was now Viscount Dundee. He led his men through Scotland, amassing support while his king besieged Derry in Ireland. Graham's men met those of King William at Killiecrankie on 27 July 1689. It was to be a victory for the Jacobites, but one tinged with disaster, as their leader was shot and killed.

> *Come fill up my cup, come fill up my can,*
> *Come saddle your horses, and call up your men;*
> *Come open the West Port and let me gang free,*
> *And it's room for the bonnets of Bonny Dundee!*
> **THE POEM 'THE BONNETS OF BONNIE DUNDEE' BY**
> **WALTER SCOTT REFLECTS HOW VISCOUNT DUNDEE WAS**
> **VIEWED AS A HERO BY THE JACOBITES.**

SOLDIER'S LEAP

Following the battle of Killiecrankie, a soldier is reputed to have jumped the River Garry, at a place now called The Soldier's Leap. Redcoat Donald McBean jumped all 18 feet of the gap while being pursued by Jacobite troops.

GLENCOE MASSACRE

> *You are hereby ordered to fall upon the*
> *rebels, the MacDonalds of Glencoe, and*
> *put all to the sword under seventy.*
> **ORDERS TO CAPTAIN ROBERT CAMPBELL, 12 FEBRUARY 1692**

This massacre is one of the most infamous events in Scottish history and took place on 13 February 1692 when government troops killed at least forty members of the MacDonald clan. The troops had been ordered to punish them after the clan chief had failed to register his loyalty to King William in time. The troops were from the clan Campbell and had been given food and shelter for twelve days by the MacDonalds before the massacre took place.

DARIEN DISASTER

Darien was on the isthmus of Panama, and a scheme was devised for Scotland to establish its own colony there. It would allow goods to be transported over the narrow isthmus to the Pacific, thereby avoiding the long voyage around Cape Horn. The man behind the venture was William Paterson, who had founded the Bank of England. He could see the riches that would ensue from operating a free port in this location. The first ships sailed in 1698.

The settlers in 'New Caledonia' found they were ill-prepared and suffered greatly from disease and hunger. Without knowing the fate of the first expedition, more ships set off from Scotland. Subsequently, the new settlers were attacked and defeated by the Spanish, who did not take kindly to Scots occupying what was seen as their territory.

As King William had ordered no help to be given, many Scots blamed England for the colony's demise. The effects on the Scottish economy were considerable – around £300,000 was lost, totalling a large proportion of the Scottish economy. For Paterson, it was worse: his wife and only son had died on the expedition, along with 2,000 other Scots.

ACT OF UNION 1707

Now there's ane end of ane old song.
**JAMES OGILVY, LORD CHANCELLOR OF SCOTLAND,
ON SIGNING THE 'ENGROSSED EXEMPLIFICATION OF
THE ACT OF UNION' IN 1706**

At the beginning of the eighteenth century, there were tensions in both Scotland and England. Scottish trade had suffered as a result of English exclusion from its colonial trade, a situation which led to the Darien disaster. Anti-English feeling was strong. In England, there was concern that when Queen Anne died Scotland might turn to a Stuart monarch again. The Scots Act of Security of 1704 gave the Scottish Parliament the right to name the Scottish monarch. It could be the same as England's – but only if Scotland was given trading and religious observation rights. In 1705 the English Parliament passed the Aliens Act which made Scots aliens – unless they accepted the Hanoverian succession. War looked likely but England was engaged in fighting France and didn't want conflict with its northern neighbour. A commissioner was sent to Edinburgh to discuss a treaty and, after negotiation, an Act of Union was put to the Scottish Parliament in October 1706, which contained the following elements:

- ☒ Church of Scotland guaranteed independence

- ☒ Scots legal system kept

- ☒ Hanoverian succession accepted

- ☒ Trade access granted

- ☒ Scots Parliament to close and Scottish MPs and peers to go to Westminster

- ☒ An equivalent of £398,085 10s to be paid by England to Scotland to compensate for taking a share of England's national debt

- ☒ A new flag

The act was passed and in March 1707, despite public protests, the Scottish Parliament met for the last time.

> *We're bought and sold for English gold –*
> *Such a parcel of rogues in a nation!*
>
> **ROBERT BURNS, FROM 'SUCH A PARCEL OF**
> **ROGUES IN A NATION' (1791)**

THE 1715 JACOBITE UPRISING

Discontent with the union and the installation of unpopular monarch Hanoverian George I led to another Jacobite uprising. Twelve thousand men amassed for the 'king over the water', as the uncrowned monarch James VIII and III (James VII and II's son) was described. The Jacobites reached Preston but were defeated and the Battle of Sheriffmuir was inconclusive, despite the Jacobites outnumbering the Hanoverian forces three to one. James VIII – known as the Old Pretender – arrived in Scotland but did not linger, lasting barely a month before heading back to France. He was an uninspiring figure, who bemoaned his life's 'constant series of misfortunes'.

THE '45

When the Old Pretender's attempts came to nothing, the Jacobite torch was passed to his son and one of Scottish history's most well-known figures: Charles Edward Louis John Casimir Sylvester Severino Maria Stuart, known as the Young Pretender and more famously as Bonnie Prince Charlie.

> *I am come home.*
>
> **BONNIE PRINCE CHARLIE ON 24 JULY 1745 TO**
> **ALEXANDER MACDONALD OF BOISDALE WHO**
> **ADVISED THE PRINCE TO RETURN HOME AND NOT**
> **GO ANY FURTHER WITH HIS EXPEDITION**

When Bonnie Prince Charlie arrived in Scotland he struggled at first to find keen supporters. But eventually he gathered enough troops to march south and, on 17 September 1745, had taken Edinburgh. The government forces in Scotland under General John Cope faced up to the Jacobites near to Tranent in East Lothian where the Jacobites triumphed in a dawn attack at the Battle of Prestonpans. It inspired the folk song, 'Hey, Johnny Cope, Are Ye Waking Yet?'

> *Lord, grant that Marshal Wade*
> *May by thy mighty aid*
> *Victory bring.*
> *May he sedition hush*
> *and like a torrent rush,*
> *Rebellious Scots to crush.*

VERSE ADDED TO 'GOD SAVE THE KING' DURING
THE UPRISING. WADE WAS IN CHARGE OF THE
GOVERNMENT FORCES BUT FAILED TO INTERCEPT
THE JACOBITES ON THEIR MARCH SOUTH

The Jacobites now marched towards the real prize: London. They got as far as Derby in December when the decision was made to turn back. The promised French and English support hadn't materialised and it was said that a government agent gave misleading information to the Jacobites' war council about the size of the capital's defending force. It was not defended that heavily and the Jacobites could have reached London before larger forces could be deployed.

Bonnie Prince Charlie's men marched back north again. They met the government forces at Culloden near to Inverness on 16 April 1746, and were heavily defeated in less than an hour in the last pitched battle on British soil. As the prince was led from the field, a Highlander was heard to shout, 'Run then, you damned cowardly Italian!' He spent months on the run, including a period where he was disguised as a woman servant called Betty Burke and guided by Flora MacDonald, before sailing to France in September.

CULLODEN AFTERMATH

The British government were not content to let the matter rest and harsh measures were imposed on the Highlanders to ensure there were no further uprisings. The commander at Culloden, the Duke of Cumberland, who was a son of King George II, was given the nickname Butcher for the post-battle actions carried out by his forces. The wounded on the battlefield were given no mercy and military executions were carried out. The Jacobites saw men tried and subsequently executed – some were hung, drawn and quartered – and others transported. There was wider suppression of the clan system with bagpipe-playing, the speaking of Gaelic and the wearing of tartan being banned – except for in British army units, such as the Black Watch. The Highlands were never to be the same again.

TARTAN

Wearing tartan universally identifies someone with Scotland. The vertical and horizontal lines that form blocks of colours originate from the Highlands, where different patterns were produced according to the different localities. Nowadays distinctive tartans are assigned to individual clan names but this was not always the case. With the books of Walter Scott, the visit of George IV to Scotland in 1822 and those of Queen Victoria starting in the 1840s, Scotland came to be seen romantically, with the Highlands home to adventurous heroes and heroines. This rise in popularity came alongside a need to be identified with this romantic place and so tartans became more commonly worn. They can now be ordered for all manner of organisations and places worldwide. For example, the following each have their own tartan:

American Society of Travel Agents
Arbroath Smokies
Argentina
ASDA Walm-Mart
Bahamas
Cape Breton
Chattahoochee (River)
Confederate Memorial
Cornwall
Princess Diana Memorial
Donegal
Edinburgh and Lothian Tourist Board
European Union
FBI

Knights Templar (Scottish International)
Niagara Falls
Oklahoma
Olympic Games
Order of the Holy Sepulchre
Royal and Ancient Golf Club
Royal Canadian Mounted Police
Salvation Army
Scottish Funeral Association
Scottish Motor Trade Association
Sultanate of Oman
US Marine Corps

DID YOU KNOW?

A piece of tartan went to the moon. Astronaut Alan Bean, who was proud of his Scottish ancestry, took a piece of MacBean tartan to the moon with him on Apollo 12 in November 1969. He later presented a piece to the Clan MacBean and to St Bean's Church in Perthshire.

ENLIGHTENMENT TO PRESENT DAY

THE ENLIGHTENMENT

*Really it is admirable how many Men of Genius
this country produces at present.*
DAVID HUME, WRITING IN 1757

The Enlightenment was a period when Scots made advancements in thought and practice that were to have a huge influence on the world. Amongst its figures were James Watt, David Hume, Adam Smith, James Hutton, Joseph Black and Adam Ferguson. Here are some of the key achievements:

- Watt's work on the steam engine played a huge part in the Industrial Revolution.

- Hume's sceptical philosophy changed the way we view ethics and religion.

- Smith wrote on human behaviour and is regarded as the father of modern economics through his theories on commerce.

- Hutton altered how the very structure of the earth was viewed through his theories on how rocks were formed, in a constant process of geological change.

- Black made major developments in chemistry and physics through his discovery of latent heat and also of carbon dioxide.

- Ferguson's writings on the nature of mankind are credited with creating sociology.

⊠ In architecture, William Adam with sons Robert, John and James created buildings of classical design that are still admired today.

⊠ Thomas Telford's canals, bridges and other structures formed part of the infrastructure of an industrialising Britain.

⊠ *Encyclopaedia Britannica* was published.

> *Today it is from Scotland that we get rules of taste in all the arts, from epic poetry to gardening.*
> **VOLTAIRE, FRENCH PHILOSOPHER, WRITING IN 1762**

HIGHLAND CLEARANCES

One of the outcomes of the post-Culloden period was the abolishing of the clan chief's heritable jurisdictions. This meant they did not have the same level of control or authority over their clan members as before; for example, they were unable to raise their own armies. It also meant they did not have the sense of care or responsibility for the well-being of their people as before. From the second half of the eighteenth century, landowners wished to make their estates more profitable and so evicted their tenants to make way for sheep and later for deer. Some tenants were thrown off their properties by force. Some that stayed in the Highlands turned to fishing but the majority searched further afield. They found work in the industrialised lowlands while others boarded ships for the new worlds. The potato famine that began in 1846 exacerbated the exodus. To give an idea of the scale, between 1841 and 1861 the western Highlands saw a third of its population leave.

The situation did not go without resistance. The Battle of the Braes in Skye began when crofters were issued with eviction notices after refusing to pay rent in a dispute over pasture rights. A battle took place, with police being pelted with stones and attacked with sticks, and consequently the crofters' rights were restored.

TOBACCO, LINEN AND COTTON

After the Union of Scotland and England in 1707, it took until the middle of the eighteenth century for Scotland's economy to improve. One of the main industries was tobacco – Glasgow was its major port in Britain and, as a result, Glasgow's 'tobacco lords' became wealthy.

Tobacco was imported from America and re-exported to Europe as part of the trading system. Ships took goods to Africa which were exchanged for slaves, who were then transported to the West Indies for the sugar plantations and America for the tobacco plantations. Tobacco and also sugar were then shipped across the Atlantic.

Sugar refined in the west of Scotland was another major industry, but the American War of Independence saw the decline of the tobacco and sugar industries. The linen industry was bigger than tobacco, but was eventually overtaken by cotton and declined until the 1860s when the American Civil War ended the supply of the raw material. Subsequently, heavy industries took over.

PAISLEY PATTERN

In the nineteenth century, the town of Paisley was a major textile producer, manufacturing shawls based on designs from Kashmir. Its name is still used to describe intricate and colourful patterns.

NEW LANARK

David Dale was one of Scotland's cotton magnates, who built the large mills at New Lanark in the late eighteenth century. Dale was concerned with the welfare of his workers and provided education for those children unable to work. Dale's son-in-law Robert Owen took over the running of the mills and developed further his ideas about the well-being of his employees. New Lanark is a major tourist attraction for the area.

INDUSTRIAL REVOLUTION

Scotland's very landscape – economic, social and physical – changed forever with the advent of the Industrial Revolution. While low-level manufacturing had been carried out previously, it was nothing compared to the sheer scale of the shipbuilding, textiles, iron and steel manufacturing industries. To power the factories, mills and engineering yards, fuel was needed and it came in the shape of coal. Mines were sunk across the central belt, in Ayrshire and Fife, and all of these industries combined to employ hundreds of thousands of people. As well as Highlanders from their crofts, thousands of Irish men and women travelled to find work. The city of Glasgow experienced a huge rise in its population between 1800 and 1830, expanding from 77,000 to 200,000. As a result, those living in the 'second city of the empire' lived in cramped and disease-ridden housing.

CLYDE-BUILT

The River Clyde became the hub of a prodigious industry: shipbuilding. In yards such as John Brown's in Clydebank, Denny's in Dumbarton, and Harland and Wolff, and Fairfield's, in Govan, over 20,000 ships were 'Clyde-built' – a phrase which signified a guarantee of quality. Before the First World War a fifth of all ships in the world were built on the Clyde. The shipbuilding industry declined after the Second World War and only two yards now remain: the BAE Systems in Govan and Scotstoun. Some of the notable ships built on the Clyde were:

Cutty Sark	*QE2*
Empress of Britain	*Britannia*
Lusitania	*Waverley*
Queen Mary	HMS *Hood*
Queen Elizabeth	HMS *Repulse*

FIRST WORLD WAR

Scots fought alongside their comrades from Britain and the rest of the Commonwealth in the First World War. It is thought 148,000 Scots died. At home, two Zeppelins attacked Edinburgh on the night of 2 April 1916 and killed thirteen civilians. Women, as elsewhere in Britain, took up employment to replace the men who had left for service in the armed forces. The chief British military figure in the conflict was General Douglas Haig, who commanded the British forces in France from 1915 to 1918. Haig was from Edinburgh, where his father owned a whisky distillery.

DID YOU KNOW?

Thankful Villages were those that saw all the men who went to war return safely. Fifty-two have been identified in England and Wales but there are none in Scotland.

RED CLYDESIDE

The Industrial Revolution imposed harsh working conditions, which were sometimes the subject of protest. In 1787 the Calton

Weavers (named after an area in the east end of Glasgow) had protested for an increase in their pay. Soldiers were drafted in and six of the weavers were shot and killed.

The period from the early twentieth century onwards saw unrest. In 1915, women had successfully protested against exorbitant rent rises, and, after the First World War, company owners and government officials feared possible revolution, as had taken place in Germany and Russia. On 31 January 1919, workers gathered in Glasgow's George Square and the red flag of communism was raised at one point. The Riot Act was read and some of the workers' leaders were arrested.

SECOND WORLD WAR

The high unemployment of the 1930s Depression was alleviated with the start of the war. Scotland's industries could build the ships, engines and other material needed for the war effort. Clydebank was heavily bombed over two nights in 1941, leaving just seven houses undamaged, but overall the loss of life was less than in the First World War.

THE TARTAN PIMPERNEL

Reverend Donald Caskie was minister for the Scots Kirk in Paris and when France was invaded by Germany in 1940 he moved to Marseille, where he helped Allied military personnel escape. Although he was captured, he survived the war and returned to his ministry in the French capital.

UPPER CLYDE SHIPBUILDERS

The post-war years saw Clyde shipbuilding suffer in the face of competition from abroad. The government formed Upper Clyde Shipbuilders, which amalgamated five yards. However, in the early 1970s, they required funding which the government had withdrawn. Six thousand jobs were at risk and, instead of a strike, union leaders organised a work-in to show the viability of the yards. One of them, Jimmy Reid, gave a speech to the workers taking part in the work-in which included a memorable promise:

> *There will be no hooliganism, there will be no*
> *vandalism, there will be no bevvying because the*
> *world is watching us, and it is our responsibility*
> *to conduct ourselves with responsibility, and*
> *with dignity, and with maturity.*

The government relented and the jobs were saved.

NEW INDUSTRIES

As Scotland's heavy industries declined in the second half of the twentieth century, they were replaced in part by the service sector. In 1971, a third of jobs in Scotland were in the service sector; twenty years later it was two-thirds. Tourism played a part in this, but other industries were also developed.

Oil was discovered in the North Sea in the 1960s, but it wasn't until the following decade that its potential as a viable industry began to be realised. It transformed the economy of the north-east, particularly in Aberdeen. In twenty-five years from 1971, Grampian's population rose by 100,000 people. But it wasn't just the north-east of Scotland that benefitted: the North Sea oil and gas industry accounted for 7 per cent of Britain's GDP in 1984.

Another area that saw development was Silicon Glen, the nickname given to the central belt for its clustering of computing technology companies. Government money was put into attracting investment and this resulted in companies such as IBM and NCR setting up manufacturing plants in Scotland. Electronics accounted for almost a quarter of Scotland's exports at the start of the twenty-first century, but as foreign companies withdrew their investment, the sector declined.

DID YOU KNOW?

Grand Theft Auto was created in Dundee. The first game was developed by DMA Design, based in the city.

TOURISM

With the decline of heavy industry as both a source of income and employer, tourism has become an important sector in Scotland. Its beginnings can be traced to the writings of Walter Scott and the royal patronage of Queen Victoria, who is credited with popularising Scotland as a holiday destination with her visits to the north-east and residencies at Balmoral Castle.

In 2015, the national tourism board VisitScotland reported visitors spending £5 billion. In 2005, the Scottish government launched a campaign to promote Scotland. Its strapline was:

The best small country in the world.

The campaign was shelved after two years.

SCOTLAND'S POLITICS

Scotland had been dominated by the Liberal Party for most of the nineteenth century. In 1847, four out of five Scots (of those eligible to vote) voted Liberal. The Liberals' strength continued into the twentieth century but the party was not to retain its position.

In 1892, Keir Hardie, an ex-miner from Lanarkshire, had been elected as an independent Member of Parliament. He was involved in the establishment of the Independent Labour Party the following year and in 1900 became chairman of the Labour Representation Committee, which in 1906 became the Labour Party. In 1922, Labour won a third of the Scottish vote and twenty-nine seats in Parliament. Two years later, another Scot, Ramsay MacDonald, led the first minority Labour government at Westminster.

The Liberal vote had declined following the First World War as Labour and the Conservatives took over as the chief parties in Scotland. In 1931, the Conservatives won forty-eight out of the seventy-one seats. After the Second World War, it was only in the 1955 election that they were to have more seats than Labour, who came to dominate Scottish elections for Westminster. In 1997, the Conservatives won no seats in Scotland.

The major element of political discourse at the start of the twenty-first century was that of independence and devolution, formerly known as home rule.

DID YOU KNOW?

In 1935, a communist MP was elected in Scotland, when Willie Gallacher won the West Fife seat. He remained an MP for fifteen years.

HOME RULE

Voices began calling for Scottish home rule in the latter part of the nineteenth century, and in response the Scottish Office was created in 1885. Following the First World War and the resulting unemployment, renewed calls were made for more powers to be held by Scots over Scottish issues. The government responded by creating a cabinet post of Secretary of State for Scotland in 1926. In 1934, the Scottish National Party (SNP) was formed and eleven years later celebrated its historic first Member of Parliament. A Scottish Covenant seeking home rule received almost two million signatures in 1949. In 1950, the Stone of Destiny (which had been taken south of the border by Edward I in 1296) was removed from Westminster Abbey and driven to Scotland by those advocating home rule.

The SNP won its second-ever seat in 1967 at the Hamilton by-election and its support increased into the 1970s, winning the party eleven seats in the general election of October 1974. In 1979, a referendum was held on Scottish devolution but, despite the majority voting yes, the condition that a minimum of 40 per cent of the electorate was required to vote was not met. In 1997, another referendum was held and the majority vote was enough to secure a devolved parliament, which opened in Edinburgh in 1999.

The SNP formed a majority government in 2011 and secured a referendum on independence which saw 55 per cent vote to remain part of the United Kingdom in September 2014. The SNP continued to retain popular support, winning fifty-six out of the fifty-nine seats available in the 2015 General Election. The 2016 Scottish Parliament elections saw the SNP return to power, with sixty-three seats, although they no longer commanded an overall majority.

MY SCOTLAND
NICOLA STURGEON
First Minister of Scotland

Which three words describe Scottish people?
Generous. Tenacious. Funny.

What is your favourite place in Scotland and why?
Walking on Dunure beach near Ayr – the scenery is breathtaking and on a clear day you get great views over to Arran and the Kintyre peninsula. My grandparents had a croft there so I have many fond memories.

What do you miss most about Scotland when away?
I'm away from home a lot but it tends to be for short periods, so I rarely have enough time to miss anything. When it's a longer trip then I'll miss my husband, especially his home cooking, and my family.

What historical event has had the most impact on Scotland?
So many to choose from and it's not an easy question, so I'll go for two in more recent memory. The Scottish Parliament being reconvened in 1999

and the Independence Referendum in 2014 were monumental in changing Scotland and had a positive impact both on how the world views us but possibly on how we see ourselves as well.

Which figure from history would you most like to speak to, and what would you ask them?

I'll go for Robert Burns. As a book and poetry lover, and a huge fan of Burns' imagery and ability to speak for us all, I'd just ask him to recite some of his work. 'My Love is Like a Red, Red Rose' was played at my wedding just before my husband and I took our vows – what a treat it would be to hear it from the Bard himself!

WEATHER AND GEOGRAPHY

WEATHER

There are two seasons in Scotland:
June and winter.
BILLY CONNOLLY

With Scotland having (or suffering from) a maritime climate, positioned at the receiving end of the Atlantic, it is unsurprising that it has a reputation for wet weather. Added to the hilly terrain, low-pressure systems dump their rain on the west of the country before moving over the sunnier eastern part, which receives around a quarter of the rainfall.

RAIN

The wettest place in Britain is not in Scotland (it's Martinstown in Dorset where 27.9 cm of rain fell in a single day in 1955). Scotland does hold second place, however, as 23.8 cm of rain fell in one day in January 1974 at Sloy Main Adit on Loch Lomond in Argyll and Bute. The western Highlands are among the wettest places in Europe, with annual rainfall over 3 metres.

WIND

The windiest place in Britain is Fraserburgh, which recorded a gust of 142 mph in February 1989. This was the most powerful gust at low-level. Scotland also holds the record for high-level gusts with 173 mph measured in the Cairngorms in 1986 at a height above sea level of 4,084 feet. In a list of windiest places in Britain (based on annual average wind speed from 1981 to 2010) Scotland had eight places in the top ten.

SUNLIGHT

Ben Nevis is the dullest place in Britain, with an average of 736 hours of sunshine per year, which works out roughly at 2 hours a day. This would have been looked on longingly by the residents of Cape Wrath in January 1983 who received half an hour's sunlight in total for the whole month. They had to wait until the penultimate day of the month for it.

'TAPS AFF'

When the weather is deemed warm and sunny enough for sunbathing, the cry of 'taps aff' (tops off) is sounded.

SCOTCH MIST

Scotch mist has a physical definition – that of a mixture of drizzle and fog found on the hills and mountains, but it also can be applied to something more ephemeral.

THE LAND

Scotland's land area makes up a third of the United Kingdom's. The landscape goes from the northern wild and sparsely populated areas of the Highlands to the agricultural and rugged moorland of the Borders and Dumfries and Galloway in the south. Above them all lie the islands of Orkney and Shetland. In the east, there is the more gently undulating countryside of the Mearns, the Strathmore valley, Fife and East Lothian, and on the west are scattered the many islands of the Inner and Outer Hebrides. In the centre are the densely populated urban areas of the central belt.

Land area (square miles):	30,414
Maximum distance (miles):	275 (north to south) 154 (west to east)
Coastline (miles):	11,601

BOUNDARIES

Scotland as it is now has been in existence since the fifteenth century. The Outer Hebrides became part of Scotland in 1263 and Orkney and Shetland in 1469. The land border between Scotland and England was mostly agreed in 1237 with the Treaty of York.

The border runs for 96 miles along the River Tweed and the Cheviot Hills. This border is now settled but varied for centuries as territory was fought over. In the south-east, the River Tweed was used as the natural divide, but the official border line now reaches the North Sea coast, north of Berwick-upon-Tweed. This town has changed nationality at least thirteen times.

EXTREMITIES

On the mainland, the four extremities of Scotland are:

North   Dunnet Head
South   Mull of Galloway

| East | Peterhead |
| West | Corrachadh Mòr, Ardnamurchan |

Away from the mainland, the most northerly point is Out Stack in Shetland (north of the superbly named Muckle Flugga) and the most westerly is Rockall, 236 miles out in the Atlantic, although its nationality is disputed. St Kilda is often taken to be the most western part of Scotland.

DID YOU KNOW?

Over 70 per cent of Scotland's land area is used for agriculture, with over half of this given to rough grazing for animals.

MOUNTAINS

The bulk of Scotland's mountains lie north of the central belt in the Highlands. Mountains above 3,000 feet in height are termed Munros, after Sir Hugh Munro who categorised them in 1891. Of the 283 currently listed, the most southerly Munro is Ben Lomond, a short drive from Glasgow. Many Munro-baggers have reached the top of all the Munros – The Inaccessible Pinnacle on Sgurr Dearg in Skye's Cuillin mountain range is the only one that requires rock-climbing skills to 'bag'.

TEN HIGHEST MUNROS		
Ranking	Name	Height (feet)
1	Ben Nevis	4,411
2	Ben Macdui	4,295
3	Braeriach	4,252
4	Cairn Toul	4,236
5	Sgor an Lochain Uaine	4,127
6	Cairn Gorm	4,085
7	Aonach Beag (Nevis Range)	4,049
8	Càrn Mòr Dearg	4,012
9	Aonach Mòr	4,006
10	Ben Lawers	3,983

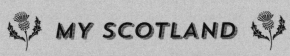

MY SCOTLAND

CAMERON MCNEISH
Writer and broadcaster

What three words describe Scottish people?

Inventive; hospitable; patient. Scotland has produced many of the world's greatest inventors and thinkers. After travelling throughout the world I can honestly say I've found few nations as welcoming as ours and Scots have to be patient to cope with our weather and our midges.

What is your favourite place in Scotland and why?

Badenoch, for the delightful mix of river, forest and mountain scenery.

What do you miss most about Scotland when away?

I miss the extraordinary diversity of our landscapes. Where else would you find the likes of the Cairngorms and the Cuillin of Skye so relatively close to each other. Or Torridon and the Angus Glen, or the Borders and the Western Isles.

What is Scotland's greatest cultural achievement?

As the birthplace of Robert Burns. His work is known and loved throughout the world.

Which figure from Scotland's past would you most like to speak to, and what would you ask them?

John Muir, who was born in Dunbar and went on to become the father of the conservation movement. I would ask him how much would he have changed Scotland if he had never moved to the US.

DID YOU KNOW?

A Corbett is a mountain that is higher than 2,500 feet, but less than the 3,000 feet of a Munro, and has a drop of 500 feet between listed hills. They are named after climber John Rooke Corbett who created the list in the 1920s. There are 222 Corbetts in Scotland.

DID YOU KNOW?

Scotland has 1,217 Marilyns. These are classed as a prominence on a hill or mountain at least 492 feet high. The name Marilyn was chosen as it complements Munro, evoking the Hollywood film star of the 1950s.

NOTABLE MOUNTAINS

Ben Nevis

At 4,411 feet Ben Nevis is the highest mountain in Britain. It is located near Fort William, in Lochaber, and forms part of the Grampians. Its name comes from the Gaelic *Beinn Nibheis* which means 'malicious mountain', although another interpretation translates the name from *Beinn nèamh-bhathais* which has a more whimsical meaning as 'mountain with its head in the clouds'.

Despite its height, 125,000 people make a successful ascent each year, bagging the highest Munro. In 1911, an unusual ascent was made when a Model T Ford was driven up the mountain as a publicity stunt. An observatory was built on the summit at the end of the nineteenth century but is now abandoned.

Buachaille Etive Mòr

High on the list of things to see when in the Highlands of Scotland is Glencoe. The famous glen offers scenic grandeur which can be seen easily without moving any distance from a visitor's car. One of its chief attractions, the dominating mountain called Buachaille Etive Mòr (Gaelic for 'the great herdsman') which guards the eastern end of the glen, can be seen while driving towards Glencoe on the A82 from Rannoch Moor. (As its name suggests, it is actually at the head of Glen Etive.) There are four peaks of Buachaille, including Stob Dearg (3,350 feet) which is the pyramidal mountain seen and photographed by many.

Ben Lomond

The most southerly Munro, Ben Lomond, rises to a height of 3,193 feet above Loch Lomond. Its proximity to the central belt makes it a popular mountain – but this doesn't take away from the views possible if the weather is clear.

Schiehallion

Schiehallion's 3,553 feet makes it an easily seen landmark for miles around. Its name translates as 'the fairy hill of the Caledonians'. The mountain was used for a successful experiment in 1774 to measure the density of the earth. A by-product of the experiment was the invention of contour lines as a way of depicting different heights of ground features.

Cairn Gorm

The mountain that gave its name to a mountain range stands 4,085 feet high. It overlooks the town of Aviemore in the

Highlands. A funicular railway opened in 2001 which takes visitors up the northern slopes.

Lochnagar

Lochnagar, also known as Beinn Chiochan (mountain of breasts), is a mountain in the Grampians. It rises to a height of 3,789 feet and one of its main features is a corrie, around which three peaks sit. While impressive in itself, it gained extra recognition when it inspired a work of verse by a famous poet of the nineteenth century. Lord Byron had spent ten years in Aberdeen as a boy – his mother was from the area – and the landscape of Scotland left a great impression on the future Romantic poet, who one day would be described as 'mad, bad and dangerous to know'. He later wrote about the mountain, and one stanza ends:

> *England! thy beauties are tame and domestic*
> *To one who has roved on the mountains afar;*
> *Oh! for the crags that are wild and majestic*
> *The steep frowning glories of dark Lochnagar*
> **FROM 'DARK LOCHNAGAR' (1807)**

Another later, also titled, visitor was the current Prince Charles, as the mountain is within the royal Balmoral estate. He too was inspired by the mountain, and published a children's book called *The Old Man of Lochnagar* in 1980.

DID YOU KNOW?

The biggest mine used in the First World War was called Lochnagar. Sixty thousand pounds of explosive were used on the first day of the Somme Offensive, on 1 July 1916.

THE DEVIL'S BEEF TUB

This memorably named feature of landscape is a hollow surrounded by four hills, located near to Moffat in Dumfries and Galloway. It is around 600 feet deep and was used to hide stolen cattle. The family thought to be behind this illicit cattle trade were described as devils. Walter Scott described it in his novel *Redgauntlet* as a 'damned deep, black, blackguard-looking abyss of a hole'.

ISLANDS

Scotland has 790 islands. Some are small and uninhabited while others have histories stretching back far in time.

ORKNEY

Seventy separate islands make up Orkney, which is blessed with some of Scotland's oldest sites:

Skara Brae

There were local stories about the Neolithic site's existence at Skaill Bay, but it wasn't until the mid 1800s when a storm blew its covering sands away that the world got to hear of it. When excavated, Skara Brae was found to be a 5,000-year-old village, complete with stone dwellings and interior furniture. Older than Stonehenge and the Pyramids it is now a must-see attraction for anyone visiting the mainland island.

Maeshowe

Maeshowe is around 4,800 years old and is the largest chambered cairn in Britain, measuring 115 feet in diameter. A 36-foot-long passageway that is about 3 feet high allows entrance to the interior burial chamber for those able to crawl or stoop. At midwinter, the setting sun shines directly up this passageway, illuminating the rear wall. In the twelfth century, Vikings looted the chamber and also left runic graffiti, some of which reads:

Ingigerth is the most beautiful of all women.
Arnfithr Matr carved these runes with this axe
owned by Gauk Trandilsson in the South land.
These runes were carved by the man most skilled
in runes in the western ocean.

Stones of Stenness
The standing stones at Stenness date from 3100 BC. Four stones are all that remain of the twelve thought to have been originally arranged. The tallest stands 19 feet high.

Ring of Brodgar
Not far from Stenness this 340-foot-diameter stone circle contains twenty-seven standing stones. The Ring is believed to be from around 2500–2000 BC.

The Tomb of the Eagles
Believed to date from around 3000 BC, this chambered tomb was discovered by a local farmer in 1958. Inside, the remains of over 300 people were found, buried over an 800-year period. Its name comes from the bones of sea eagles found there.

Hoy
Hoy is Orkney's second biggest island. To the west stands the 450-foot-high sea stack, known as the Old Man of Hoy, which was the location for a memorable live TV event in 1967 when a team that included Chris Bonington, Dougal Haston and Hamish MacInnes climbed it. An estimated 15 million viewers watched.

DID YOU KNOW?

The First World War German fleet ended its days in Orkney. Following the end of the war, the ships were escorted to Scapa Flow, but on 21 June 1919 the crews deliberately sank fifty-two of their own vessels. All but seven were refloated and salvaged.

SHETLAND

Shetland is 600 miles north of London and 400 miles south of the Arctic Circle. The nearest part of Scotland is Orkney, 50 miles away. Shetland is made up of more than a hundred islands, fifteen of which are inhabited. The islands span a distance of 100 miles north to south.

Humans have lived on Shetland for about 6,000 years with the Vikings arriving in the eighth century. The Norse influence is readily apparent through place names and words that form part of the local dialect, stemming from the ancient Norn language which was spoken on Shetland (as well as Orkney) until Scots took over. Shetland only became part of Scotland in 1472. Lerwick is the main town and half the total population live within 10 miles.

DIALECT WORDS	
simmer dim	period of almost constant daylight during summer nights
peerie smoorikins	little kisses
taamie norie	puffin

neesik	porpoise
blinnd moorie	snowstorm
mirry dancers	Northern Lights
gaffin	laughing
blyde	glad
filsket	excited
vargin	working in tough conditions
wirset gansey	wool jumper
trowie people	trolls

Up Helly Aa

This fire festival is a torchlight procession through Lerwick, led by the Guizer Jarl and his Jarl Squad dressed in elaborate Viking costumes, which ends by setting fire to a Viking longboat. It began in its current guise in the 1880s.

Jarlshof

This site in the southern end of Shetland's mainland contains historical artefacts from the Neolithic, Bronze Age, Iron Age, Pictish, Viking, and medieval periods and also from the sixteenth century. In a similar event to that in Skara Brae in Orkney, a storm blew away the sands that had covered the site in the late nineteenth century.

Broch of Mousa

This broch (round tower) dates from the Iron Age, around 100 BC. It is located on the small island of Mousa and is one of the best preserved brochs of the period.

Foula

Foula is one of Scotland's remotest inhabited islands, lying 20 miles west of Shetland's mainland. Around twenty people live on the island, which has no shop or pub and is served by aircraft and a small ferry service, both heavily dependent on the weather. The people of Foula celebrate the festive period at different times from the rest of Scotland. Christmas is marked on 6 January and New Year a week later as these are dates from the Julian calendar which was kept when the rest of the country moved to the Gregorian calendar in 1752.

Fair Isle

Vying with Foula to be the most remote inhabited island, Fair Isle has dramatic sea cliffs and a large sea-bird population but it is the Fair Isle jumper that has made the island world-famous.

St Ninian's Isle

St Ninian's was the location for a major treasure find in 1958. During excavations of the chapel, a hoard of eighth-century silver was discovered by a schoolboy. It is now on show in Edinburgh.

DID YOU KNOW?

Shetland's capital Lerwick is closer to Bergen in Norway than to Edinburgh.

OTHER ISLANDS

Some of Scotland's other notable islands include:

Arran	Described as 'Scotland in miniature', Arran has land features similar to those in different parts of Scotland. Its highest peak, Goat Fell, is only 134 feet short of being a Munro. A distillery was established in 1995 and a brewery has been making beer since 2000.
Skye	Skye's major feature is the Cuillin mountain range. The island was joined to the mainland by a road bridge, opened in 1995. There was controversy over the tolls, which were removed in 2004.
Mull	Tobermory, in Mull, known for its brightly painted buildings, attained a level of fame when the children's TV show *Balamory* was filmed in the town. It also gave its name to the bowler-hatted Womble who helped Great Uncle Bulgaria in the 1970s TV programme.
Lewis and Harris	Lewis is the northern part of the island Lewis and Harris (which are often thought of as separate islands). In 1831, a hoard of twelfth-century carved chess pieces were found on a beach, and given the collective name of the Lewis Chessmen. The most notable visitor attraction in Lewis is the Callanish Stones, dating back 5,000 years and predating Stonehenge. Harris is famous worldwide for its Harris Tweed clothing fabric. It is also known for its scenic beaches, with two notable ones at Luskentyre and Scarista.

St Kilda	Sitting 66 miles west of Benbecula, this group of islands make up the St Kilda archipelago. Hirta has been inhabited since the Neolithic period but is now uninhabited, save for personnel at a military base. In 1930, the last islander left for the mainland. In each cottage, an unlit fire was set in the grate and a Bible was left open at Exodus. The cliffs at Conachair are Britain's highest, at 1,410 feet. St Kilda also has the highest sea stack: Stac an Armin is 643 feet high.
Bute	Bute is in the Firth of Clyde. Its only town is Rothesay, and was a popular location for tourists who came 'doon the watter' from Glasgow and the west coast. The main route to Bute is the ferry from Wemyss Bay. Another ferry trip connects Bute to the mainland – a 330-yard journey from the north of the island to the Cowal peninsula. One of Bute's main visitor attractions is the ornate Mount Stuart House.
Eriskay	This small island was the location for a pivotal moment in Scottish history when Bonnie Prince Charlie stepped onto Scottish soil for the very first time. The Hebridean island found fame again two centuries later when a cargo ship carrying a quarter of a million bottles of whisky ran aground. The fate of the SS *Politician* was turned into a novel and a film called *Whisky Galore!*.

Islay	Islay is famous for its whisky – there are eight distilleries on the island. Bowmore has been distilling the 'water of life' since 1779.
Staffa	This uninhabited island a few miles west of Mull is famous for its columns of basalt rock and Fingal's Cave, which inspired an overture by German composer Felix Mendelssohn.
Bass Rock	Home to a large colony of gannets, which number around 150,000, the Rock was also home to a seventh-century hermit called Baldred. The inactive volcano was also used as a prison for Covenanters.
Inchmickery	One of the islands in the Firth of Forth. Military fortifications were built here during the First World War and are said to resemble a naval vessel in outline.
Gruinard	This small island off the west coast between Gairloch and Ullapool was used as a testing ground for biological warfare. In the Second World War anthrax was released and its effects on animals were monitored. The resulting contamination meant the island was closed to visitors for half a century.

DID YOU KNOW?

In 1934, a German rocketeer attempted to deliver mail from the island of Scarp to Harris, but the rocket exploded and the 1,200 letters on board were scattered to the winds.

Speed, bonnie boat, like a bird on the wing,
Onward! the sailors cry;
Carry the lad that's born to be King
Over the sea to Skye.

'THE SKYE BOAT SONG' WAS WRITTEN ABOUT THE JOURNEY OF BONNIE PRINCE CHARLIE FROM UIST TO SKYE WHEN HE WAS BEING PURSUED BY BRITISH GOVERNMENT SOLDIERS

COAST

Scotland faces the Atlantic Ocean in the west and the North Sea in the east. Its coast ranges from wide, sandy beaches to rugged cliffs and everything in between. Despite its relatively large landmass you are never more than 50 miles from the sea and 70 per cent of the Scottish population live within 6 miles of the coast.

DID YOU KNOW?

Scotland makes up 8 per cent of Europe's coastline.

DID YOU KNOW?

Two-thirds of all the fish caught in British waters are landed in Scotland.

CORRYVRECKAN WHIRLPOOL

This large whirlpool is located between the isles of Jura and Scarba. Boat trips can take visitors but care should always be exercised; in 1947, George Orwell and his family almost drowned in the whirlpool when his boat's engine failed.

BEACHES

Scotland's beaches rank alongside any in the world with crystal clear water and breathtaking scenery. Five of Scotland's best beaches are:

Luskentyre Beach

The white sands and turquoise waters combine with a beautiful setting on the west coast of south Harris to make Luskentyre a regular feature on lists of Britain's best beaches.

West Sands, St Andrews

The 2-mile-long sands would be familiar to viewers of the 1981 film *Chariots of Fire*.

Silver Sands of Morar

The beaches at Morar also starred in a film. *Local Hero*, written and directed by Bill Forsyth, and released in 1983, is about an American oil company wishing to build an oil refinery on the site of a local village and several scenes were filmed there. The isles of Rum, Eigg and Muck can be seen offshore.

Sandwood Bay
The beach at Sandwood Bay in north-west Sutherland is not easily accessible and requires a 4-mile walk but its unspoilt sands mark it as one of the best beaches in Britain. A 240-foot-high sea stack called Am Buachaille (The Herdsman) sits at its southern end.

Machir Bay, Islay
Many ships have been wrecked on the rocks around Islay and the wreck of one can be seen in the sands at Machir Bay, one of Islay's best beaches. The sands run for over a mile.

DUNBAR'S BRIDGE TO NOWHERE
Visitors to the beach at Dunbar at high tide would be bemused to see a bridge that is stuck in the water, with no way of reaching it without swimming. The bridge is intended for use at low tide when it allows beachgoers to cross the Biel Water which runs out to sea. A visitor who times it wrongly can expect a long walk back to the town.

MACHAIR
This grassy, low-lying terrain can be found on Orkney, Shetland, and the north and western Highlands – half of all the machair is in the Outer Hebrides. It is mostly composed of broken sea shells. The beaches of the east coast have a higher mineral content.

DID YOU KNOW?

Scotland has its own bridge over the Atlantic. The small island of Seil was connected to the Scottish mainland by a stone bridge in 1792. The Clachan Bridge was designed by Thomas Telford (see page 252 for more on Telford).

RIVERS

Given the plentiful supply of rain, Scotland's rivers are well-supplied and form a dynamic part of the landscape.

RIVER TAY
Length: 119 miles
This is Scotland's longest river and runs from Ben Lui near Tyndrum in the Highlands, then through Loch Tay, before reaching Perth, Dundee and the North Sea. The Tay contains more water than the Thames and Severn together.

RIVER SPEY
Length: 100 miles
The Spey begins appropriately at Loch Spey in the Highlands and flows down towards the Moray Firth. Speyside is known for its whisky production and salmon fishing.

RIVER CLYDE
Length: 106 miles
It rises in the Lowther Hills of South Lanarkshire, at 1,550 feet above sea level, and runs through the city of Glasgow. The river

was the main driver for the city's economic and industrial rise, and 'Clyde-built' became a byword for quality in shipbuilding.

RIVER TWEED
Length: 96 miles
This natural border between Scotland and England passes the home of the Borders' most famous son, Walter Scott, at Abbotsford.

RIVER DEE
Length: 96 miles
The Dee rises in the Grampians and follows an easterly route through Deeside before reaching the harbour area of Aberdeen. It is another Scottish river well known for its salmon fishing.

RIVER DON
Length: 82 miles
The Don rises in the Grampians near to Cock Bridge and meanders through Aberdeenshire before entering the North Sea, north of Old Aberdeen. The river gives its name to Aberdeen's football team, the Dons, being one of Scotland's more successful sides.

RIVER FORTH
Length: 55 miles
The Forth starts in the Trossachs and runs through Aberfoyle and Stirling before becoming an estuary. In 2008, the Clackmannanshire Bridge opened, which is the fourth Forth estuary crossing. The Queensferry Crossing road bridge opened in 2017.

LOCHS

The lochs of Scotland are an essential part of its landscape. There are over 31,000 freshwater lochs in Scotland, and a number of sea lochs are on the west coast. One of the lochs has a very famous resident.

LOCH NESS

Without the lure of the mythical creature, the loch is interesting in itself. It is the biggest body of fresh water in Britain, holding almost twice as much water as all of the lakes of England and Wales combined, and is 23 miles long. Although it has a smaller surface area than Loch Lomond, its volume is larger. Its deepest point is 755 feet below the surface – deep enough to hold almost four of Edinburgh's Scott Monuments standing on top of each other.

The dark water claimed the life of British racer John Cobb in 1952 during a world record attempt. Cobb, who had held the world land-speed record, was travelling at over 200 miles an hour in his jet-powered boat *Crusader* when it nosedived into the water.

DID YOU KNOW?

There is a loch in Scotland that looks like Scotland. Viewing Loch Garry from the A87 north of Fort William makes the shape of the loch resemble that of Scotland's mainland.

LOCH MORAR

Scotland's deepest freshwater loch is in Lochaber in the western Highlands. Its maximum depth is 1,017 feet. Along with Loch Ness, it is rumoured to have its own mysterious creature. Morar's is called Morag.

LOCH LOMOND

Loch Lomond has the largest surface area of fresh water in Britain. Its maximum dimensions are 24 miles in length and 5 miles wide. Ben Lomond rises from the eastern banks.

DID YOU KNOW?

The first National Park in Scotland was Loch Lomond and Trossachs, opened in 2002.

Oh you'll tak' the high road,
and I'll tak' the low road,
And I'll be in Scotland afore ye,
But me and my true love will never meet again,
On the bonnie, bonnie banks of Loch Lomond.
'THE BONNIE BANKS O' LOCH LOMOND'

This song of loss, the chorus of which is reproduced above, has been sung for hundreds of years. There are several explanations for the lyrics, with some claiming they're the feelings of a Jacobite prisoner imprisoned in England.

DID YOU KNOW?

A colony of wallabies lives on one of Loch Lomond's islands. These mammals were introduced to Inchconnachan in the 1940s.

SEA LOCHS

One of the notable features of Scotland's west coast is its sea lochs, which are similar in nature to the fjords of Norway. They provide special habitats for over 1,700 species of marine life. Some of the lochs include:

Loch Carron	Loch Long
Loch Crinan	Loch Maddy
Loch Eriboll	Loch Ranza
Loch Ewe	Loch Ryan
Loch Fyne	Loch Seaforth
Loch Leven	Loch Sunart
Loch Linnhe	Loch Torridon

GARDENS

Gardening is as popular in Scotland as the rest of Britain and this interest is complemented by large-scale gardens that are popular attractions.

DAWYCK BOTANIC GARDEN

Dawyck is a woodland garden, located 8 miles from Peebles. Two trails take visitors through one of the great collections of rare trees and shrubs. Plants have been grown here for 300 years, including some brought back by Scottish botanist David Douglas from his travels in North America. One of the trails is named in his honour.

ROYAL BOTANIC GARDEN EDINBURGH
The gardens in Edinburgh are one of the most popular attractions in the city and are regarded as an oasis of calm in the capital. The garden was founded in 1670.

GLASGOW BOTANIC GARDENS
Situated in Glasgow's West End, the botanic gardens were established in Kelvinside in 1842 and provide a pleasant space for Glaswegians. The Kibble Palace is one of the glasshouses in the gardens.

INVEREWE GARDEN
You wouldn't expect to find a tropical garden in Wester Ross but that's what Inverewe is. Created in 1862, the garden at the southern end of Loch Ewe is full of exotic plants, such as Himalayan blue poppies, Tasmanian eucalyptus trees and Nepalese rhododendrons. The plants thrive due to the Gulf Stream's warm currents and the protection of pines which were planted for this purpose.

CITIES AND TOWNS

From the early days of the burghs, which were established to allow trading, Scotland's towns and cities have developed their own unique characteristics. This allows rivalries to exist between some of the cities and the joke told by Aberdonians – 'What's the best thing about Dundee? The road out' – has also been applied to others.

Scotland has six officially recognised cities:

ABERDEEN

Nickname: The Granite City, The Silver City

Population: 228,990 (as of 2014)

Rivers: Don, Dee

Famous citizens: Annie Lennox, Thomas Blake Glover, Lord Byron, Denis Law

Football teams: Aberdeen, Cove Rangers

Aberdeen is Scotland's third largest city. There's evidence that humans have lived there for around 8,000 years and it is thought that the Roman settlement of Devana was on the site of the present city.

Situated on the north-east coast, Aberdeen's harbour made it a natural place for trade, and its history as a trading burgh goes back to the twelfth century. The city's economy is now dominated by the oil and gas sector, owing to its nearness to the drilling fields in the North Sea. The harbour was once filled with fishing boats; while the industry has since declined, it remains an important part of the economy.

NOTABLE BUILDINGS

St Nicholas' Church

This kirk dates back to the twelfth century but has been extensively developed since. The spire is 196 feet high. Inside it has the largest carillon in Britain with forty-eight bells, one of which weighs 4.6 tons. Despite being a religious site for all its time in existence, during the Jacobite rebellion the Duke of Cumberland used the church to stable his troops' horses.

DID YOU KNOW?

Aberdeen has won the Britain in Bloom horticultural competition a record ten times.

St Machar's Cathedral

St Machar's holds a unique position: it is the only medieval church made of granite in the world. Located in the Old Aberdeen area of the city, it dates back to the twelfth century. It is claimed that following his execution in London in 1305, parts of William Wallace's body were placed within the walls of the cathedral. Sections were destroyed following the Reformation of 1560 and a storm in 1688 brought down the tower. The structure had been weakened when Oliver Cromwell's soldiers removed stones to build a military fortification in 1650.

Town House
The town house – built of granite, of course – stands at the eastern end of Union Street. It was completed in 1873 and its tall spire serves as a landmark in the city. The previous town house now serves as a visitor gateway to the university.

Marischal College
The world's second largest building made of granite is the current headquarters of Aberdeen City Council, but it began life in the 1830s as part of Aberdeen's second university. In 1860 Marischal College (founded in 1593) merged with King's College (founded in 1494) to form Aberdeen University. The building was extended in 1906 and is now 400 feet long and 80 feet high.

DID YOU KNOW?

The oldest company still in existence in Britain is the Aberdeen Harbour Board, which was established by King David I in 1136.

DUNDEE

Nickname: None

Population: 148,260 (as of 2014)

River: Tay

Famous citizens: Brian Cox, A. L. Kennedy, Ricky Ross, George Galloway, Billy MacKenzie, Eddie Mair, John Graham, Mary Slessor

Football teams: Dundee, Dundee United

Dundee is a city that has one of the best locations in Scotland. It faces onto the wide estuary of the River Tay with the Lomond Hills of Fife beyond. The city itself rises up towards Dundee Law, an extinct volcano that reaches a height of 572 feet and gives a panoramic view of the surrounding landscapes and the 'silvery Tay'.

Its history is similar to many other Scottish towns in that there have been periods of English invasion and civil war causing destruction. It is thought as much as a fifth of the population was killed during the siege by Cromwell's New Model Army in 1651.

Established as a burgh in the twelfth century, Dundee exported wool and animal hides to Europe and imported grain and wine. In terms of importance it stood alongside Edinburgh, Aberdeen and Perth in the fourteenth century and was to become more so over the years as its overseas trade was supplemented by the making of cloth – one of the key industries that led eventually to Dundee being labelled as the city for jute, jam and journalism.

The nineteenth-century jute industry exported large amounts of the material. The effects of this large-scale industry were seen on the human population: the workers needed for the factories and mills led to overcrowding and unsanitary housing conditions. As a result, Dundee had the highest levels of child mortality in Scotland by the end of the nineteenth century. Whaling and shipbuilding were other large industries. One of the ships built in Dundee was the *Terra Nova* which took Captain Scott to the Antarctic in 1910.

The second J – jam, in the form of marmalade – did not account for a large proportion of the workforce and neither did journalism, which was most visibly seen in the output of publisher D. C. Thomson in papers such as *The Courier* and the *Sunday Post*.

The city has had to adjust to post-industrialisation and has seen much change and development. Almost all the pre-eighteenth-century buildings are no longer in existence. During the radical urban development of the 1960s and 1970s many old buildings and structures were lost, including the grand Victoria Arch in the docks area, which was demolished to make way for the new road bridge.

DID YOU KNOW?

Men in Dundee were historically known as kettle-boilers, as women made up two-thirds of the workforce in the jute and linen industries and the men were left to look after the domestic duties.

NOTABLE BUILDINGS

Gardyne's House
This burgess house on the high street is hidden from obvious view but offers a rare opportunity to see a sixteenth-century building still standing in the city.

The Old Steeple/St Mary's
The original church in the Nethergate was destroyed by Edward I. Rebuilt two centuries later, it was destroyed again in 1548. It was rebuilt later in the sixteenth century and a square tower was constructed, which is known as the Old Steeple and gives its name to one of the Church of Scotland's congregations that shares the building. Its other name is Dundee Parish Church (St Mary's).

Caird Hall
The city's prosperous years made its mill owners very wealthy and some of this money was put back into the city through benevolence. The Caird Hall, which opened in 1923, was financed by one of the jute magnates, Sir James Key Caird, and is one of the city's most recognisable buildings.

DID YOU KNOW?

Dundee has been Moscow. For the filming of Alan Bennett's play *An Englishman Abroad* the Caird Hall's large Doric-columned frontage was draped with communist banners from the Soviet Union. The play is about Cambridge spy Guy Burgess who fled to the Soviet Union in the 1950s.

Other notable locations:

Dundee Law
The Law (never the Law Hill, as 'law' means hill in Scots) dominates the city. Evidence of human habitation from around 1500 BC has been found.

Discovery
This wooden ship was used by Captain Scott and Ernest Shackleton on their first Antarctic expedition between 1901 and 1904. It gave rise to the city's punning tourism slogan: City of Discovery.

Gates
Dundee is filled with streets that end in 'gate': Cowgate, Flukergate, Marketgate, Murraygate, Nethergate, Overgate, Seagate, Stannergate, Wellgate.

DID YOU KNOW?

Winston Churchill served as MP for Dundee for fourteen years, between 1908 and 1922.

DID YOU KNOW?

Dundee's two football teams – Dundee and Dundee United – are situated 200 yards apart. Dens Park and Tannadice are both located on the city's Sandeman Street and are the closest grounds in British football.

EDINBURGH

Nickname: Auld Reekie, Athens of the North

Population: 492,680 (as of 2014)

River: Water of Leith

Famous citizens: Sean Connery, Robert Louis Stevenson, Craig and Charlie Reid, Arthur Conan Doyle, Chris Hoy, James Young Simpson, James Boswell, Ronnie Corbett, Harry Lauder, Muriel Spark, Walter Scott, Irvine Welsh, Alexander Graham Bell, James Hutton, James Clark Maxwell

Football teams: Heart of Midlothian, Hibernian, Edinburgh City

Beautiful city of Edinburgh! the truth to express,
Your beauties are matchless I must confess,
And which no one dare gainsay,
But that you are the grandest city in
Scotland at the present day!
WILLIAM MCGONAGALL

Scotland's capital, Edinburgh's compact city centre, featuring many historical sites, natural features and surroundings, makes it a popular place for visitors from around the world. Described as 'Scotia's darling seat' by Robert Burns, Edinburgh sits south of the Firth of Forth and looks north towards Fife, with the Pentland Hills providing a backdrop to the south.

Edinburgh's origins go at least as far back as the Mesolithic era. The city became a royal burgh in the early part of the twelfth century and under King James IV it became the capital of the country. Following the disaster of the Battle of Flodden, the defensive Flodden Wall was built around the city.

It gained the name Auld Reekie – meaning 'old smokie' – because of the fug issuing from the many domestic fires used for heating and boiling water. In the 1700s the overcrowded population of around 40,000 were concentrated along the main thoroughfare, running from the castle down the Royal Mile to Holyrood Palace. It was not a pleasant place to live and dwellings were stacked up alongside each other: some went up fourteen storeys.

In 1752, a pamphlet, written with the support of the city's Lord Provost, was published entitled *Proposals for Carrying on a Certain Public Work in the City of Edinburgh*, which, among other improvements, aimed to 'enlarge and beautify the town, by opening new streets to the north and south, removing the markets and shambles'. This would help develop prosperity and encourage 'people of rank' to reside in the city. It led to the New Town being built.

NOTABLE BUILDINGS

Edinburgh Castle

The castle occupies a commanding position above Edinburgh's city centre. Originally constructed of wood, the stone buildings on the site date back to the twelfth century. Each year, at the end of the Edinburgh Festival and at Hogmanay, a spectacular fireworks display uses the castle's ramparts as its launching point.

Balmoral Hotel

Since its opening in 1902, the Balmoral holds pride of place at the corner of Princes Street and North Bridge, next to Waverley Station. The clock on its dominant tower is helpfully set 3 minutes fast, to ensure passengers are in time for their trains. Author J. K. Rowling finished *Harry Potter and the Deathly Hallows*, the last novel in the series, in room 552. Other celebrities to have stayed at the hotel include Laurel and Hardy, Paul McCartney and Beyoncé.

St Giles' Cathedral
A church has stood on this site on the Royal Mile since the twelfth century. St Giles' is the High Kirk of Edinburgh and its crown-shaped spire is one of the Edinburgh skyline's most recognisable features.

Scottish Parliament
Scotland's own parliament was suspended following the Act of Union in 1707, but in 1997 the Labour government began moves to resurrect it. A devolution referendum was held that year and Scots voters chose to have their own parliament. Elections were held in May 1999 and the first sitting was held in the Church of Scotland's General Assembly Hall on the Mound.

A new parliament was built at the bottom of the Royal Mile on the site of an old brewery. The parliament's design and construction were mired in difficulties, with changes being made to architect Enric Miralles' original vision, resulting in delays and cost overruns. The final building cost £414 million and was opened three years late in October 2004.

Holyrood Palace
The name Holyrood stems from the old Scots phrase *haly ruid* meaning 'holy cross'. In 1128, King David I dedicated an abbey there, and a supposed relic of the True Cross, which had been passed down from David's mother, Queen Margaret, was kept at the abbey. The palace that was built on the site by James IV became the main royal residence in 1542, and is still used by the present-day royal family.

Other places of interest:

Arthur's Seat

Of Edinburgh's seven hills, the biggest is Arthur's Seat. To some it resembles a resting elephant and its 823-foot-high summit is visible for miles around. It affords the best vantage point in the city and a visit to Edinburgh is not complete without a trek to the top. The extinct volcano forms part of Holyrood Park and its other geological feature, the cliffs of Salisbury Crags, also offer a dramatic physical feature for a capital city.

Scott Monument

The largest monument to a writer in the world stands proudly on Princes Street. The statue of the pre-eminent Scottish nineteenth-century novelist Walter Scott is made of Binny sandstone and stands 200 feet high, with 287 steps awaiting the non-claustrophobic, non-vertiginous visitor.

DID YOU KNOW?

In 2004, Edinburgh became the world's first UNESCO City of Literature.

Calton Hill

Calton Hill sits above the eastern end of Princes Street. The Nelson monument marks the achievements of the famous admiral who orchestrated victory at the Battle of Trafalgar in 1805, at which he sustained fatal injuries. Another architectural feature is the National Monument of Scotland, a planned memorial to those Scots who died defeating Napoleon. Started in 1826, the project ran out of money and 'Edinburgh's Disgrace' remains incomplete.

Heart of Midlothian

A section of the pavement near to St Giles' has cobbles set in the shape of a heart, which were laid to mark the position of the city's Old Tolbooth, which was demolished in 1817. The Tolbooth was used for tax collection and as a prison – there is a tradition in Edinburgh of spitting on the heart, which may be a sign of disdain for the site's past.

DID YOU KNOW?

During the eighteenth century, at 10 p.m. each evening, cries of 'Gardyloo!' would be heard from the high tenement buildings. The Scottish version of *Garde l'eau* (Watch out, water) was a warning that the waste material collected during the day was about to be thrown out of windows and down onto the streets – and onto any unfortunate passers-by. The waste lay uncollected until the next morning.

New Town

Starting from the 1770s, Edinburgh began building what became known as the New Town. (Centuries later it retains this moniker.) Streets to the north of the castle and the Nor Loch were built on carefully laid out lines – later described by Robert Louis Stevenson, who lived in Heriot Row, as 'draughty parallelograms' – with long streets running east to west bisected by perpendicular ones. Squares and crescents were included. These streets were given names reflecting the city's loyalty to the Hanoverian monarchs, such as:

- Princes Street

- Queen Street

- George Street

- Great King Street

- Hanover Street

- Cumberland Street (George III's son, the Duke of Cumberland)

- Charlotte Square (George III's wife)

- Frederick Street (George III's father)

Bridges were also constructed: North Bridge, connecting the Old Town to the New Town, was opened in 1772. It was replaced by a steel bridge a century later. Another route to connect the city's two main parts was the Mound, which was built on top of excavated earth from the New Town works. The National Gallery of Scotland and the Royal Scottish Academy were built on the Mound. The Old Town slums were cleared in the latter part of the nineteenth century, but a feeling for what life was like in the Old Town can be experienced in many places, especially on a dark and foggy winter's night.

DID YOU KNOW?

Following a trend for neoclassical architecture, Edinburgh styled itself as the 'Athens of the North' in the nineteenth century.

You'll have had your tea.

THE TRADITIONAL GREETING ISSUED BY AN EDINBURGHER ON RECEIVING AN UNEXPECTED GUEST AROUND TEATIME

INTERCITY RIVALRY

It is fair to say that there is a degree of rivalry and mutual distrust between some residents of Scotland's two largest cities, situated at either end of the M8 motorway. The term weegie, used in the capital to describe their westerly compatriots is rarely heard in Glasgow, which is probably lucky for the speaker intending on using it. Billy Connolly once said that Edinburgh is on the other side of the world – if you go the wrong way.

You'll have more fun at a Glasgow stabbing than an Edinburgh wedding.

CHEWIN' THE FAT (BBC SCOTLAND)

GLASGOW

Nickname: The Dear Green Place

Population: 599,650 (as of 2014)

Rivers: Clyde, Kelvin

Famous citizens: Charles Rennie Mackintosh, Billy Connolly, Peter Capaldi, James McAvoy, Gerard Butler, Robert Carlyle, Midge Ure, Frankie Boyle, Robbie Coltrane, Rikki Fulton, Armando Iannucci, Lorraine Kelly, Kenny Dalglish, Alex Ferguson, Alexander 'Greek' Thomson

Football teams: Celtic, Rangers, Partick Thistle, Queen's Park

Glasgow is Scotland's largest city. It began as a settlement founded by Saint Mungo (also known as Kentigern) around AD 550 and grew hugely in the Industrial Revolution when heavy industry burgeoned. The resultant overcrowding and accompanying disease and ill health took decades to be overcome. Modernisation began in the 1960s, in which time many of the old tenements were pulled down and their residents moved to large tower blocks – the multis. Social ties were lost as many of the tower-block estates were not provided with suitable amenities.

While it might not have the kudos of being the capital, its inhabitants bow to no one in being proud of their city. A 1980s publicity campaign used the Mr Happy character from the *Mr Men* series of books, accompanied by the slogan 'Glasgow's miles better', which attracted much attention and helped kick-start the city's revival.

NOTABLE BUILDINGS

Glasgow Cathedral

The cathedral is situated on the site of a church built by Saint Mungo and is one of Glasgow's most impressive buildings. It measures 285 feet long and its spire rises 225 feet. It was consecrated in 1197 and the building as we know it today was completed in the fourteenth century. Unlike many other churches in Scotland, it escaped destruction in the Reformation when local tradesmen united to defend it.

Kelvingrove Art Gallery and Museum

Kelvingrove has one of the best municipal art collections in Britain and is a much-loved institution in the city. An urban myth has it that this fine red sandstone building was built back to front and that the architect, distraught on seeing his project ruined, ran up to the top and jumped off the roof.

City Chambers

Glasgow's municipal headquarters is a grand building that fills one end of the city centre's George Square. It was completed in 1888 and opened by Queen Victoria.

DID YOU KNOW?

In 1999 improvement work on Glasgow's Kingston Bridge saw the 52,000-ton structure raised by 1.5 cm, to allow new concrete piers to be built underneath. Over 155,000 vehicles cross the River Clyde over the bridge each day.

Provand's Lordship
Glasgow's oldest house, Provand's Lordship, is located near to the city's cathedral. It was built in 1471 as part of a hospital and is one of only four medieval buildings that still exist in the city. It is maintained by Glasgow museums and can be visited by the public.

Glasgow School of Art
The school was designed by Charles Rennie Mackintosh (see page 156) and completed in 1909. It is probably the best example of Mackintosh's exterior and interior architectural vision. A fire in 2014 caused major damage to this iconic building.

Mitchell Library
Named after Stephen Mitchell, a tobacco merchant who left a large part of his estate to fund it, this library opened in 1911 and is Europe's largest.

Armadillo
Officially the Clyde Auditorium, the Armadillo was built next to the Scottish Exhibition and Conference Centre beside the River Clyde and opened in 1997. Although the design was intended to reflect the shipbuilding area in which it was located, with curved metal sides representing ships' hulls, it gained the nickname of a South American mammal.

DID YOU KNOW?

In 1981, Glasgow was the first city to grant Nelson Mandela a freedom-of-the-city honour. After he was released, he came to the city to accept the honour in 1993, a year before he became President of South Africa.

Traffic Cone Statue

For years it has been a common occurrence to see a traffic cone sitting on top of a statue in Glasgow's city centre. The Duke of Wellington outside the Gallery of Modern Art in Royal Exchange Square is the recipient of the ritual which has become an unofficial landmark of the city.

> *Here is the bird that never flew.*
> *Here is the tree that never grew.*
> *Here is the bell that never rang.*
> *Here is the fish that never swam.*

THIS VERSE WAS INSPIRED BY THE MIRACLES
SAINT MUNGO REPUTEDLY PERFORMED AND
INFLUENCED GLASGOW'S COAT OF ARMS

INVERNESS

Nickname: Inversnecky

Population: 56,660 (as of 2014)

River: Ness

Famous citizens: Karen Gillan, Charles Kennedy, Jessie Kesson, Ali Smith

Football team: Inverness Caledonian Thistle

Situated at the top of the Great Glen, Inverness is known as the Capital of the Highlands. Pictish kings lived in the area from the fifth century and it was on Craig Phadrig to the west of the city that King Bridei had his fort. The legend goes that when Columba arrived the king denied him access, but the future saint opened the locked gates by simply knocking. This impressed Bridei so much he is said to have immediately converted to Christianity.

Occupying an important geographic location, Inverness saw more than its fair share of conflict over the centuries, but in 2014 a survey found it to be the happiest place to live in Scotland, and second happiest in Britain.

NOTABLE BUILDINGS

Eden Court Theatre
Eden Court was opened in 1976 and, following its development in 2007, is now the largest venue for theatre, cinema, dance and other arts in Scotland.

Inverness Castle
The current castle was built in 1834. It occupies a prominent position above the River Ness and is now used as the area's Sheriff Court.

St Andrews Cathedral
The Scottish mainland's most northerly cathedral sits on the banks of the River Ness. It first opened its doors in 1869.

Town House
The Victorian-Gothic Town House was the headquarters of the burgh of Inverness and now holds offices for the Highland Council. In 1921 it was the venue for a historic occasion when the British Cabinet met for the first time outside of London. Prime Minister David Lloyd George was on holiday in the Highlands and did not wish to return to London.

Market Bar

Despite its tiny stage, this legendary music venue has held gigs by many singers and bands, including The Proclaimers, who in their early days used to travel up from Edinburgh by bus.

DID YOU KNOW?

It is claimed that Invernessians speak clearer English than in any other part of Scotland.

STIRLING

Nickname: Gateway to the Highlands

Population: 91,580 (as of 2014)

River: Forth

Famous citizens: Billy Bremner, Kirsty Young, Kenny Logan, Willie Carson

Football team: Stirling Albion

Who does not know its noble rock, rising, the monarch of the landscape, its majestic and picturesque towers, its splendid plain, its amphitheatre of mountain, and the windings of its marvellous river.

JOHN MACCULLOCH, SCOTTISH GEOLOGIST, WRITING ON STIRLING IN 1824

Stirling became a burgh in the twelfth century, a status it kept until burghs were done away with in the local government reorganisation of the 1970s.

Its heritage is plain to see in the medieval Old Town, which is dominated by the castle. Stirling occupies the lowest crossing point of the River Forth and was therefore of huge strategic value. It is thought the castle was besieged sixteen times as a result. Nowadays it is only besieged by visitors: almost half a million a year.

DID YOU KNOW?

British racing driver Stirling Moss was named after the city his mother came from.

NOTABLE BUILDINGS

Stirling Castle

The castle sits at the top of the Old Town and is the major visitor attraction in the area. King James V was known to go from the castle to mingle with the common people in the guise of the 'guid man' of Ballengeich – Ballengeich being a pathway leading down from the castle.

Church of the Holy Rude

Although the church was founded in 1129, the current building dates back to the fifteenth century. It is the city's second oldest building after the castle. James VI was crowned here in 1567.

Mar's Wark
This ruin was once home to the Earl of Mar (*wark* is a Scottish word for building).

Argyll's Lodging
Described by Historic Environment Scotland as 'the most important surviving town-house of its period in Scotland', this seventeenth-century building sits close to the castle and was occupied, as the name suggests, by the Earls of Argyll. It is now the site of a museum.

DID YOU KNOW?

When the University of Stirling was founded in 1967, it was Scotland's first university for 400 years.

TOWNS AND VILLAGES

BALLATER, BRAEMAR AND BALMORAL
These towns are all located in Deeside – often known as Royal Deeside as it came to prominence following the visits of Queen Victoria in the nineteenth century. Victoria would arrive at the train station at Ballater on her way to her Balmoral estate. It is claimed that because she didn't want trains going past her royal residence she prevented the train line continuing west and so it never reached Braemar.

Braemar is the coldest place in Britain, reaching a lowest-ever temperature of minus 27.2 degrees Celsius in January 1982 (and also in 1895). The Braemar Gathering is the Highland Games that is regularly attended by members of the Royal Family.

The gathering has its roots going back hundreds of years to King Malcolm III's time when he evaluated his fittest soldiers.

LAIRD OF CANDACRAIG

Comedian Billy Connolly became Laird of Candacraig when he bought Candacraig House in Deeside in 1998. As laird he would attend the local Lonach Gathering and invited Hollywood stars such as Judi Dench, Ewan McGregor, Eric Idle, Steve Martin and Robin Williams, the latter of whom not only appeared in full Highland dress, but also took part in the hill race.

DID YOU KNOW?

The shortest place name in Scotland has two letters: Ae in Dumfries and Galloway.

DULL AND BORING

The Perthshire village of Dull is twinned with a similarly themed named town in Oregon: Boring. The ninth of August has been declared Dull and Boring Day in the US state.

SCOTLAND'S CALIFORNIA

California is a small village near Falkirk. The self-proclaimed Sunshine Village was formerly populated by miners, working at the nearby collieries. Scotland also has a Moscow (in Ayrshire).

BRECHIN 'CITY'

Although the football team is Brechin City, Brechin, with its population of just over 7,000, is actually a town. The 'city' comes from it having a cathedral and an accompanying diocese but this designation is no longer valid. Elgin City Football Club is also given this name on the same basis.

TOWN'S NICKNAMES

Many Scottish towns have nicknames, the origins of which are not always known:

Polo Mint City	East Kilbride (it has a lot of circular roundabouts)
Auld Grey Toun	Dunfermline, St Andrews, Hawick
Blue Toun	Peterhead (from the blue gaiters fishermen wore)
The Broch	Fraserburgh (an old Scots word for burgh)
Fair City	Perth
Honest Toun	Musselburgh
Lang Toun	Auchterarder, Darvel, Kirkcaldy
Muckle Toun	Langholm
Shaky Toun	Comrie (situated on the Highland Boundary Fault Line)
Wee Red Toun	Kirriemuir (due to the red bricks used in the town's houses)

CULROSS

Culross in Fife contains a collection of buildings that were built in the seventeenth century. On one of the buildings a plaque has been placed with an unusual inscription: 'In this spot in 1832 nothing happened'.

DID YOU KNOW?

The north-east fishing town of Fraserburgh was also known as Little London because of the high number of bombs that fell on it in the Second World War.

Auld Ayr, wham ne'er a town surpasses,
for honest men and bonnie lasses.
ROBERT BURNS, 'TAM O' SHANTER' (1791)

FLORA AND FAUNA

Scotland's wildlife is a mix of distinctive indigenous species and more common animals and plants that can be seen in the rest of Britain. Despite the desire of many visitors to see one in the flesh, it is not possible to see a wild haggis (they are furtive creatures who shy away from any attempts at observation). However, this still leaves much to be enjoyed in Scotland's outdoors.

FLORA

HEATHER
Scotland's mighty mountains and moorland are covered by this tenacious plant that can live for up to forty years. It produces a pink or purple flower which can be seen from late summer.

SCOTTISH BLUEBELL
From spring to early summer, woodlands can be carpeted in the glorious blue of the Scottish bluebell, also known as the harebell.

SCOTS PINE

This evergreen conifer can live for 700 years. Its timber is noted for its strength and is used to make telegraph poles. In 2014 it was voted Scotland's national tree.

DOUGLAS FIR

This species of evergreen conifer was named after the Scottish botanist David Douglas who travelled in North America in the early part of the nineteenth century. He sent samples home and introduced over 200 species to Britain.

DID YOU KNOW?

Douglas firs can live to be 1,000 years old. The coastal varieties can grow to a height of 250 feet.

SEA BINDWEED

This plant was said to have been introduced to the beach at Eriskay when seeds fell out of the pocket of Bonnie Prince Charlie when he arrived in 1745. As the plant is also found on Orkney, where the Jacobite prince never visited, it is likely to be just a story.

FORTINGALL YEW

This yew tree in the churchyard at Fortingall in Perthshire is said to be between 2,000 and 5,000 years old. Although it has lost much of its structure, it is still a living tree.

MEIKLEOUR BEECH HEDGE

This Perthshire hedge is the longest, and tallest, in the world. At its maximum it measures 120 feet high and runs for a third of a mile. It was planted in 1745 by a woman of the area called Jean Mercer and her husband. When he died at Culloden she left for Edinburgh and it is believed she gave instructions for the hedge to be left to grow towards heaven as a memorial to her departed husband.

SCOTS NAMES

Many species have been given their own Scottish common names:

Bloody fingers	foxglove
Bull's bags	green-winged orchid
Cat's lugs (ears)	cotton grass
Cockaloorie	daisy
Granny's mutch (cap)	columbine
Hairy Davie	mint
Mammy flowers	forget-me-not
Poor man's clover	selfheal
Sleepin' Maggie	stock
Sticky Willie	goose grass

DID YOU KNOW?

The weed ground elder is called bishop's weed after the religious difficulties of the sixteenth and seventeenth centuries, during which the very idea of bishops in the Church of Scotland was contentious.

FAUNA

There are certain species which are hugely identified with Scotland – no visit would be complete without sight of a Highland cow – although one of them is not too popular with visitors or locals despite the myriad of preventative sprays and ointments available in Highland shops. The midge might bring discomfort to some, but there's much more to Scottish wildlife than this pesky insect.

BIRDS

Scottish Crossbill
This member of the finch family is the only endemic species of bird in Britain, i.e. it is not found anywhere else in the world. They can be seen in the Highlands.

Crested Tit
Limited to pinewood habitats in the Highlands, the crested tit is easily identified by its distinctive looking black-and-white crest markings.

Capercaillie
The capercaillie is part of the grouse family and in Britain is only found in Scotland. It was reintroduced following extinction in the eighteenth century but is again at risk. The male of the capercaillie is known for the unusual sounds it makes when demonstrating its status to other males.

Great Auk
The great auk became extinct in Britain in 1840 when the last surviving bird of this flightless species was captured and killed by men from St Kilda. They thought it was a witch.

Osprey

This bird of prey was reintroduced to Scotland in 1954 after becoming extinct in 1916. Barbed wire had to be put around nesting sites to prevent egg collectors stealing the rare eggs.

INSECTS

Midge

The midge is the scourge of anyone relishing the outdoor life during summer. Swarms of the wee blighters can clear a campsite in seconds. *Culicoides impunctatus*, the Highland midge, accounts for 90 per cent of human bites. Although they are only a seventeenth of an inch (1.5 mm) long, their bite can result in an inflamed area that will last for several days.

Scottish Wood Ant

The Scottish wood ant is one of two wood ant species in Scotland. It is mostly found in the Highlands.

Mountain Bumblebee

This species of bee (also known as the bilberry or blaeberry bumblebee, as it lives near to this type of shrub) can be seen in Scotland, but its numbers are in decline.

Rannoch Looper

A butterfly found in central Scotland but has habitats in Russia, Japan and North America.

MAMMALS

Highland Cow

The Highland cow is regarded around the world as a symbol of Scotland. With their long, shaggy hair and sharp horns, they can be seen anywhere in the Highlands. 'Hielan' coos' have two layers of hair, helping them survive the cold winters.

Deer

The proud stag is another of Scotland's iconic symbols. There are four species in Scotland:

1. Red – one of Scotland's native species, the red deer is the biggest wild mammal that can be seen on land. They are found in woodlands or on tops of mountains.

2. Roe – the second native species, roe deer are the most common. They are sometimes seen in the parks of Scotland's major cities.

3. Fallow – this non-native species was introduced to Scotland from England and also found its way into the natural habitat through escaping from deer parks.

4. Sika – originating from Japan, sika were introduced to Scotland in the nineteenth century. Their interbreeding with red deer poses a threat to the purity of the species.

St Kilda Species

Soay sheep were introduced to the St Kildan island of Soay in the Bronze Age. A hardy species, they are a third the size of other sheep. Another breed of sheep, the Boreray, were kept on the island of the same name and, due to their low numbers, are the rarest breed of sheep in Britain. Other species found only on St Kilda are the St Kilda wren, St Kilda house mouse and St Kilda field mouse. Following the evacuation of 1930, the house mouse became extinct.

Shetland Pony
The Shetland pony reaches a height of 3 feet and 6 inches. These small mammals live in fields on Shetland but their diminutive size meant they were once seen pulling coal out of the coal mines on the British mainland.

Red Squirrel
Featuring in many Scottish calendars, the red squirrel is under threat from a foreign invader in the shape of the American grey squirrel. Several organisations have set up campaigns to protect this iconic symbol of the Scottish natural habitat.

Pine Marten
At the start of the twentieth century, this member of the weasel family was limited to habitats in the north-west of the country, but it has enjoyed a healthy period since and can be found as far south as the central belt, and some were introduced to Galloway.

Wildcat
The last species of British cat living in the wild, the wildcat has European-protected status. It is an elusive animal – so much so that accurate numbers of how many survive are difficult to determine. Like the pine marten, they are only found in the Highlands.

Beaver
Beavers became extinct in Scotland around four centuries ago, but in 2009 Eurasian (European) beavers were reintroduced at Knapdale Forest in mid-Argyll. It was the first legal reintroduction of any species in Britain.

SCOTS NAMES

As with flora, many species of fauna have been given their own Scottish common names:

Bonxie	great skua
Clegg	horsefly
Clock leddy	ladybird
Corbie	crow or raven
Cushie-doo	wood pigeon
Devil's darning needle	dragonfly
Foggie toddler	common carder bee
Goloch	beetle
Jenny Gray	wren
Jenny-lang-legs	crane fly
Lang Sandy	heron
Mason's ghost	robin
Peewit	lapwing
Puddock	frog
Stankie	moorhen

DID YOU KNOW?

The last wolf to be killed in Scotland was shot in 1743.

NOTABLE ANIMALS

Some very well-known animals have lived in Scotland:

Greyfriars Bobby

The most famous Scottish animal is a Skye terrier that gained worldwide fame for faithfully standing by the grave of his master for fourteen years. A bronze statue of Bobby stands near the gates of Greyfriars Kirk and visitors are known to touch his nose for luck, although the origin of this tradition is unknown and no special good fortune has been attributed to Bobby.

Wojtek

Wojtek was a Syrian brown bear taken into the care of Polish soldiers during the Second World War. When the troops were in Italy, Wojtek found a role in moving artillery ammunition, leading to his unit adopting a bear carrying an artillery shell as part of their badge design. After the war Wojtek was taken to Edinburgh Zoo, where he was a popular attraction. He died in 1963.

Dolly

Dolly was born in 1996 and was the world's first successfully cloned mammal from an adult cell. The work was carried out by the Roslin Institute outside Edinburgh. She was put down in 2003 after it was discovered she was suffering from an incurable lung disease. She was given the name of American country and western singer Dolly Parton as the source of her DNA was from a mammary gland.

Maxwell's Otters

Nature writer Gavin Maxwell's 1960 book *Ring of Bright Water* tells of one man's relationship with nature and, in particular, with otters he looked after. Maxwell lived at Sandaig, in the west Highlands, which he called Camusfearna in the book. After spending time in Iraq, he had brought back an otter which he called Mijbil. It was later identified as belonging to a new sub-species and given the name *Lutrogale perspicillata maxwelli*.

Mijbil was killed by a workman, and another otter that Maxwell looked after died in the fire that destroyed Maxwell's cottage. He wrote several other books but none had the impact – or sales – of this 1960 classic, which was later made into a film.

THE ARTS

Scotland's artists, writers, musicians and performers have enriched the cultural world. Its most famous poet is still recited over 200 years since his death and any visitor to Scotland's capital city will not fail to see a giant city-centre memorial to its most famous novelist.

DID YOU KNOW?

Glasgow was the UK's first European Capital of Culture, in 1990. It followed Paris, Berlin, Amsterdam, Florence and Athens. Liverpool was the next British city, in 2008.

LITERATURE

The stories and history of Scotland provided the material for Walter Scott, Scotland's most prominent novelist of his age and for years afterwards. The country's dramatic landscape and its people would continue to provide inspiration for generations of writers although there would be a world of difference between the romanticised glens of Scott and the gritty urban Edinburgh of Irvine Welsh.

GREAT SCOT
WALTER SCOTT (1771–1832)

It is difficult sometimes to grasp how renowned Walter Scott was in his lifetime. A novelist, poet, playwright, historian and much more besides, Scott altered the way his country viewed itself and was viewed from outside. He created a Scotland full of mythology, adding a layer of mystique to a land beset by economic and political hardship. His writings helped shape the Scots' feelings about their history and gave them a sense of pride. Scott's major works include poems *The Lay of the Last Minstrel*, *The Lady of the Lake* and *Marmion* and novels such as *Waverley*, *Rob Roy*, *Redgauntlet*, *The Bride of Lammermoor*, *The Antiquary*, *Old Mortality*, *The Heart of Midlothian* and *Ivanhoe*.

Scott is regarded as having created the genre of the historical novel, and his bestselling and influential epic poem of 1810, *The Lady of the Lake*, is credited with popularising the Trossachs as a tourist destination.

When his publisher was declared bankrupt in 1826, Scott became liable for debts of £121,000. He resolved to literally write off these debts and the effort he put into this is believed to have shortened his life: he died in 1832.

GREAT SCOT
ROBERT LOUIS STEVENSON (1850–94)

Stevenson was born in Edinburgh in 1850 and studied law at the city's university before turning his hand to writing. His reputation was established with the publication of *Treasure Island* in 1883 and he went on to write classic stories such as *The Strange Case of Dr Jekyll and Mr Hyde* and *Kidnapped*. In 1888 he began a period of travelling around the Pacific islands. Bedevilled by ill health through much of his life, he died of tuberculosis in 1894 in Samoa.

SCOTLAND'S FAVOURITE BOOK

In 2016 the BBC held a vote to find viewers' favourite Scottish books. They announced the winners in October of that year:

Sunset Song	This 1932 novel by Lewis Grassic Gibbon tells of a farming community in the north-east of Scotland through the experiences of a young farmer's daughter, Chris Guthrie.
The Wasp Factory	Iain Banks' first novel is set on a remote Scottish island and is told from the perspective of a troubled teenager called Frank Cauldhame (Scots for cold home). Frank's psychopathic brother Eric has escaped from a secure institution and is returning home.

Lanark: A Life in Four Books	Alasdair Gray's 1981 masterpiece, a book that took thirty years to write from inception to publication, is seen as an important novel in Scotland's literary canon. The four books contained within *Lanark* combine autobiographical experiences of studying at the Glasgow School of Art with an allegorical tale of a young man, the eponymous Lanark.
The Thirty-Nine Steps	This classic adventure tale by John Buchan was published in 1915. The hero is Richard Hannay, who attempts to foil a plot in the summer of 1914 by a German spy ring called the Black Stone. Buchan's novel has been filmed several times.
The Prime of Miss Jean Brodie	Muriel Spark's novel about an Edinburgh teacher and her teaching of six girls – the crème de la crème – at the Marcia Blaine School for Girls is set in the pre-war 1930s. It features regularly in lists of all-time great novels.
Harry Potter and the Philosopher's Stone	J. K. Rowling began her successful series about the boy wizard with this novel, published in 1997. She said the inspiration came to her while on a train and the formula of good versus evil proved hugely successful in print and subsequent films.

Trainspotting	Irvine Welsh's tales of Begbie, Renton, Sick Boy and Spud showed the side of Edinburgh the tourist authorities might not want highlighted: heroin addiction on council estates.
Knots & Crosses	Ian Rankin's highly successful crime novels feature the hard-drinking, authority-defying detective John Rebus. *Knots & Crosses* was the first of the series.
The Adventures of Sherlock Holmes	This book of short stories featuring the legendary detective and his assistant Watson was published in 1892. Its writer, Edinburgh-born Arthur Conan Doyle, wished to concentrate on other projects and killed off Holmes at the hands of his nemesis Moriarty in 1893 but relented and wrote more adventures until 1927.
The Private Memoirs and Confessions of a Justified Sinner	In early nineteenth-century Scotland, James Hogg was well-known for his poems, but this 1824 novel was not greatly received at the time. It gained recognition in the twentieth century and has been cited as an influence on Robert Louis Stevenson's *Dr Jekyll and Mr Hyde*.

MY SCOTLAND

IAN RANKIN
Author

Which three words describe Scottish people?
Industrious; inventive; thrawn.

What is your favourite place in Scotland and why?
Tough question. I always enjoy my visits to the Oxford Bar in Edinburgh. But the road from Ullapool to Tongue is jaw-dropping. And I love walking the shoreline in and around Cromarty.

What do you miss most about Scotland when away?
I miss things like a good fish supper (salt and sauce please), the chat in the pubs, *Still Game* on TV, Irn-Bru...

What is Scotland's greatest cultural achievement?
Our greatest cultural achievement? There are so many. Sir Walter Scott more or less invented the historical novel; Conan Doyle gave the world its greatest detective; Logie Baird; Jekyll and Hyde; Miss Jean Brodie; Harry Potter. Did you know Scots featured in the original line-ups of The Beatles and the Rolling Stones?

> *Which figure from Scotland's past would you most like to speak to, and what would you ask them?*
>
> I'd love to ask Robert Louis Stevenson what was in the original version of Jekyll and Hyde. He burnt it after his partner Fanny said she didn't like it.

THE DAN BROWN CODE

Following his success with his bestselling novel *The Da Vinci Code*, American writer Dan Brown stayed at the Witchery on Castle Hill in Edinburgh. Before he checked out he wrote on the wooden floor his signature and a number: 93065. This riddle has yet to be solved.

HARRY POTTER'S SCOTLAND

Author J. K. Rowling was living in Scotland when she wrote the seven novels in the *Harry Potter* series. When she began, she would often use cafes to write. One was in Edinburgh on Nicolson Street. Scotland also plays a part in the books:

- Hogwarts School of Witchcraft and Wizardry – the school where Harry meets Ron and Hermione is located in the Highlands.

- Professor Minerva McGonagall is head of Gryffindor house – she grew up in the Highlands and was the daughter of a Presbyterian minister and a witch.

❌ Wigtown Wanderers – the Dumfries and Galloway town has a Quidditch team named after it. Wigtown is renowned for its book festival and is styled Scotland's National Book Town.

With the success of the books it was inevitable that films would be made and this allowed Scotland again to feature in them. Among the locations used are Glenfinnan Viaduct, Loch Shiel, Loch Etive, Glencoe and Rannoch Moor.

ORWELL IN JURA

In 1946 the writer George Orwell began living on the Hebridean isle of Jura in order to concentrate on a novel he was writing on a future dystopian Britain. Battling ill health (which was diagnosed as tuberculosis), he lived in the austere environment of a farmhouse called Barnhill on the northern part of the island. There was no electricity and he had to rely on help from his sister Avril. He left the island to be treated in hospital in East Kilbride and enjoyed a respite. With his publisher expecting delivery of his book, he was forced to return to Jura to complete the novel and it was finished at the end of 1948. He returned to the mainland and the book *Nineteen Eighty-Four* was published in June 1949. Orwell was not able to enjoy the success of his book: he died in January 1950.

DID YOU KNOW?

Ratty, Mole, Mr Toad and Mr Badger were from Scotland. *Wind in the Willows* author Kenneth Grahame was born in Edinburgh in 1859. He became the secretary of the Bank of England but it was as a writer that he made his name, when his story of the four animals was published in 1908. Another children's classic to have its origins in Scotland was *The Tale of Peter Rabbit*. Beatrix Potter spent many childhood summers in Perthshire and the book was written while she was there. The character Mrs Tiggy-winkle is believed to be based on a local woman called Kitty MacDonald.

COMICS

D. C. THOMSON

Many of Britain's best-loved comic-book characters hail from one publisher: D. C. Thomson of Dundee. It is responsible for Dennis the Menace (and Gnasher), Lord Snooty, Roger the Dodger, Desperate Dan, Minnie the Minx, Alf Tupper (the Tough of the Track) and the Bash Street Kids among many others. Their exploits in the *Victor*, *Dandy* and *Beano* comics were read by millions of children.

The company also produced two icons of Scottish culture: The Broons and Oor Wullie. The Broons are a large family of Granpaw, Paw and Maw and their children Hen, Daphne, Joe, Maggie, Horace, the Twins and the Bairn, who, despite being introduced in 1936, have never died nor aged. They live in a tenement flat in 10 Glebe Street in the fictional town of Auchenshoogle. The Broons have an annual devoted to them, which alternates every year with another lovable character from the same town: Oor Wullie. In his trademark dungarees, Wullie is always up to mischief with his pals Fat Bob, Wee Eck and Soapy Soutar, but nothing too damaging ever occurs.

DID YOU KNOW?

In 2004 a buyer paid £20,350 for a comic – a first edition of *The Dandy* from 1937. This was the highest auction price ever paid for a British comic.

GRAPHIC NOVELS

Scotland's contribution to the world of comics is not limited to those from Dundee. Grant Morrison has written for DC Comics' superheroes Batman and Superman and Marvel's Fantastic Four and X-Men as well as producing his own creations. He has collaborated with fellow Scot Mark Millar, who has also carved out a career writing for major comic-book publishers.

DID YOU KNOW?

The *Scots Magazine* is the oldest magazine in the world, founded in 1739 and still published today. It includes articles of Scottish interest on food, people, culture, history and places to visit.

POETRY

BLIND HARRY

Blind Harry was a fifteenth-century poet who wrote *The Actes and Deidis of the Illustre and Vallyeant Campioun Schir William Wallace* (*The Acts and Deeds of the Illustrious and Valiant Champion Sir William Wallace*) which was 12,000 lines in length. Written a century and a half after its subject had died, there are many historical inaccuracies.

OSSIAN

In the 1760s James Macpherson published several works that he claimed to be written by the third-century Celtic poet and warrior Ossian. They received wide acclaim not just in Scotland but in Europe as well – Napoleon carried a copy with him. However, there were strong doubts as to the veracity of the authorship.

GREAT SCOT
ROBERT BURNS (1759–96)

Burns is Scotland's bard. His poems and songs are read and sung to this day: most noticeably, a rendition of his 'Auld Lang Syne' is performed at New Year's parties around the world. He was of farming stock and continued to work the land while he wrote his poetry – one of his most famous works, 'To a Mouse', begins with a farmer's plough upsetting a mouse's nest.

Burns' first book of poetry was published in 1786 and was met with wide acclaim. He wrote his poems in Scots and English but it was in Scots that he was best able to express his views of the world. In 'To a Mouse' he wrote:

But Mousie, thou are no thy-lane,*
In proving foresight may be vain:
The best laid schemes o' Mice an' Men,
Gang aft agley,
An' lea'e us nought but grief an' pain,
For promis'd joy!

His creative output was not enough to prevent him from always needing gainful employment and after farming he became an excise officer. The toil of his early life eventually caught up with him and he died of heart problems in 1796.

Burns liked the company of men and women and was able to combine this love of physical pleasure with a mind looking beyond the hills of Ayrshire and Dumfries and Galloway to all of humanity. This was best expressed in his 1795 song 'A Man's a Man for a' That'. The song ends:

For a' that, an' a' that,
It's coming yet for a' that,
That Man to Man, the world o'er,
Shall brothers be for a' that.

These are some of Burns' most memorable works:

POEMS

- ☒ 'Tam o' Shanter'

- ☒ 'John Anderson, my Jo'

- ☒ 'To a Mouse'

---

*   alone

- ✖ 'Holy Willie's Prayer'
- ✖ 'The Cotter's Saturday Night'

SONGS

- ✖ 'Ae Fond Kiss'
- ✖ 'Auld Lang Syne'
- ✖ 'A Man's a Man for a' That'
- ✖ 'Scots Wha Hae'
- ✖ 'A Red, Red Rose'

BURNS AND SCOTT

Robert Burns and Walter Scott met, but only once. Scott was a fifteen-year-old student and Burns was making his first visit to Edinburgh. The meeting took place at the home of Professor Adam Ferguson. Scott later wrote of Burns:

> *His person was strong and robust: his manners rustic, not clownish; a sort of dignified plainness and simplicity, which received part of its effect perhaps from one's knowledge of his extraordinary talents.*

Both men contributed to a renewed sense of Scottish self-esteem, by portraying Scots, both contemporary and historical, in an attractive light. It is a sad parallel that both men, born in different social circumstances, would end their days broken by work, their talents with the pen not being enough to give them a comfortable enough existence to see them through the difficulties they faced.

MAKARS

Since 2004 Scotland has had a Makar – a national poet for Scotland, similar in role to the Poet Laureate in England. There have been three so far:

2004–10	Edwin Morgan
2011–16	Liz Lochhead
2016–20	Jackie Kay

Other notable Scots poets include Norman MacCaig, whose works in English celebrated many aspects of Scotland including the beauty of the Highlands; Sorley MacLean, regarded as the most important Gaelic poet; Sydney Goodsir Smith, who, despite not being a native Scots speaker, wrote his finest works in Scots; Iain Crichton Smith, who was a prolific writer, in English and Gaelic, of poetry, novels and plays; Orkney-born Edwin Muir, who was a major figure in the Scottish Renaissance; and fellow Orcadian George Mackay Brown, who wrote novels and poems of life and the culture of the islands.

In Scotland, when people congregate, they tend to argue and discuss and reason; in Orkney, they tell stories.
GEORGE MACKAY BROWN

GREAT SCOT
HUGH MACDIARMID (1892–1978)

Hugh MacDiarmid (the pen name of Christopher Murray Grieve) was a major figure in the rejuvenation of Scottish culture and literature in the early twentieth century. He worked as a journalist, but after serving in the army during the First World War he dedicated himself to promoting the causes he supported such as socialism and the expression of Scottish culture, which he felt was being lost. To these ends he founded several literary periodicals and was involved in the formation of the National Party of Scotland in 1928, which became part of the Scottish National Party in 1934.

His long-form poem *A Drunk Man Looks at the Thistle* was published in 1926 and is regarded as his masterpiece. In the 2,685-line poem MacDiarmid looks at subjects including Scottish identity and the situation he finds himself being 'whaur extremes meet'.

ART

Scotland's free public galleries hold works of fine art representing many periods by the great names of artistic expression and are an inspiration for aspiring art students. Among the works held in the main collections of Edinburgh and Glasgow are:

GLASGOW MUSEUMS	NATIONAL GALLERIES OF SCOTLAND, EDINBURGH
A Man in Armour (1655) Rembrandt van Rijn	*The Murder of David Rizzio* (1833) William Allan
The Last of the Clan (1865) Thomas Faed	*The Monarch of the Glen* (1851) Edwin Landseer
Christ of St John of the Cross (1951) Salvador Dalí	*The Porteous Mob* (1855) James Drummond
Interior: The Orange Blind (*c.*1927) F. C. B. Cadell	*The Storm* (1890) William McTaggart

The Reapers (1860) Jules Breton	*The Hunt* (*c*.1926) Robert Burns
View of Ventimiglia (1884) Claude Monet	*Haystacks: Snow Effect* (1891) Claude Monet
The Tuileries Gardens, Paris (1900) Camille Pissarro	*The Reverend Robert Walker* *Skating on Duddingston* *Loch* (*c*.1795) Henry Raeburn

SCOTTISH ART

There have been four groups of artists from the late nineteenth century to the present day that have contributed massively to the image and reputation of the country's artistic landscape.

The Glasgow Boys

The Glasgow Boys was a name given to a loose group of around twenty innovative artists, whose peak period of creativity was in the 1880s and 1890s. They were known for bringing a new style of naturalistic painting to Scottish art, inspired by J. M. Whistler and painters on the Continent, such as Jules Bastien-Lepage and J. F. Millet. They employed strong use of colour and light; to begin with they tended to work outside and their subject matter heavily featured rural scenes. Later they depicted the inhabitants of Glasgow's affluent suburbs. Eventually, colour, texture and pattern came to be more important. Among the group were:

☒ James Guthrie (1859–1930)

☒ John Lavery (1856–1941)

- ⊠ E. A. Walton (1860–1922)

- ⊠ E. A. Hornel (1864–1933)

- ⊠ Joseph Crawhall (1861–1913)

- ⊠ Arthur Melville (1858–1904)

- ⊠ James Paterson (1854–1932)

- ⊠ George Henry (1858–1943)

- ⊠ William Kennedy (1859–1918)

- ⊠ W. Y. Macgregor (1853–1923)

Some key works:

- ⊠ *A Highland Funeral* (1882) by James Guthrie

- ⊠ *To Pastures New* (1883) by James Guthrie

- ⊠ *A Hind's Daughter* (1883) by James Guthrie

- ⊠ *The Tennis Party* (1885) by John Lavery

- ⊠ *The Druids – Bringing in the Mistletoe* (1890) by George Henry and E. A. Hornel

The Glasgow Girls
Active from the 1890s to 1920, this was a group of female artists who all studied at the Glasgow School of Art. They were part

of the Glasgow style, an avant-garde design movement inspired by the Arts and Crafts Movement as well as Art Nouveau and Symbolism. It had been instigated by The Four: sisters Margaret and Frances Macdonald and their respective husbands Charles Rennie Mackintosh and Mackintosh's architect and artist colleague Herbert MacNair. Other members of the movement were Jessie M. King, Annie French, Bessie MacNicol, Jessie Newbery, Ann Macbeth, Norah Neilson Gray, De Courcy Lewthwaite Dewar, Stansmore Dean and Eleanor Allen Moore. A retrospective exhibition of their work was part of the programme of Glasgow's Year of Culture in 1990 and more recently an exhibition of their work was held at Kirkcudbright Town Hall and Glasgow School of Art in 2010. Some of the movement's key works are:

- *The White Rose and the Red Rose* (1902) by Margaret Macdonald

- *The High History of the Holy Graal* (1903) illustrated by Jessie M. King

- *The Silk Dress* (*c.*1911) by Eleanor Allen Moore

- *The Choice* (*c.*1909–15) by Frances Macdonald

- *A Belgian Refugee* (*c.*1915–21) by Norah Neilson Gray

Scottish Colourists

The eye seeks refreshment in painting.
Give it joy not mourning.
LESLIE HUNTER

The Scottish Colourists were a group of artists consisting of S. J. Peploe, J. D. Fergusson, Leslie Hunter and F. C. B. Cadell. They were active in the first part of the twentieth century. The term for this group was coined in the 1940s, when only one (Fergusson) was still alive. Although grouped together, they used different styles and didn't work collaboratively like the Glasgow Boys, although they did follow them in looking to the Continent for inspiration, from artists such as the post-impressionist Cezanne and the Fauves Matisse and Derain. They are known for their still lives and landscapes, with bold use of colour as a key element. Some key works are:

- *Les Eus* (*c.*1910) by J. D. Fergusson

- *The Brown Crock* (*c.*1925) by S. J. Peploe

- *Interior: The Orange Blind* (1927) by F. C. B. Cadell

- *Houseboats, Loch Lomond* (*c.*1930) by Leslie Hunter

New Glasgow Boys

This was a group of figurative artists who studied at the Glasgow School of Art in the late 1970s and early 1980s. They were Ken Currie, Peter Howson, Adrian Wiszniewski and Steven Campbell. Currie's bleak and haunting scenes of social deprivation mirror those of Howson, whose early work featured strong portrayals of working-class men. They are in contrast to Wiszniewski's colourful and lyrical scenes and Campbell's more playful surrealistic paintings. Some key works:

- *A Man Perceived by a Flea* (1985) by Steven Campbell

- *Weeds in a Landscape* (1989) by Adrian Wiszniewski

- ☒ *Patriots* (1991) by Peter Howson

- ☒ *The Bathers* (1992–3) by Ken Currie

GREAT SCOT
CHARLES RENNIE MACKINTOSH (1868-1928)

Mackintosh's famous building is the Glasgow School of Art, but other examples of his architectural skills can be found in Scotland Street School and Hill House in Helensburgh. He combined architectural work with original decorative art and furniture design. However, his talent did not result in a sustained career in architecture in Glasgow. With his wife, Margaret Macdonald, who was a great influence on his life and work, he lived in Suffolk, London, and the south of France, where Mackintosh's aptitude in watercolour painting was expressed. He died in 1928 of cancer. In the latter part of the twentieth century his talents came to be appreciated much more than during his life and an industry grew up inspired by his designs, producing some items which were described as Mockintosh.

> *Art is the Flower. Life is the Green Leaf. Let every artist strive to make his flower a beautiful living thing, something that will convince the world that there may be, there are, things more precious more beautiful – more lasting than life itself.*
> **CHARLES RENNIE MACKINTOSH**

PUBLIC ART

The traveller around Scotland can view some interesting public artworks, all available to see for free.

The Kelpies

The Kelpies are giant steel sculptures of two horses' heads. They were constructed from over 900 stainless-steel plates and rise to a height of 98 feet in their location close to the M9 motorway near Falkirk. *The Kelpies* were designed by artist Andy Scott as 'monuments to the horse and a paean to the lost industries of the Falkirk area and of Scotland'. Completed in 2013, they were modelled on Clydesdale horses, the workhorses used extensively in the Industrial Revolution. The kelpie is a mythical water spirit, often described as being in the form of a horse.

The Horn

Any driver who uses the M8 motorway between Glasgow and Edinburgh will be aware of a stainless-steel structure beside the road near Whitburn in West Lothian. The object is *The Horn*, designed by Matthew Dalziel and Louise Scullion, and installed in 1997. The 97-foot-high object – which some have compared to the Voice Trumpets in the children's TV show *Teletubbies* – was used to broadcast music, sounds and poetry, although the audio part no longer operates.

Big Heids

Designed by David Mach, these three artworks stand 33 feet high, placed close to the A8 dual-carriageway near the Eurocentral distribution centre outside Glasgow. They are built from converted shipping containers and the 'heids', made of steel tubes welded together, were modelled on local men and women.

Sawtooth Ramps

On the north side of the M8 motorway near Bathgate, seven pyramid-shaped earthwork ramps are part of the M8 Art Project that included the *Big Heids* and *The Horn*. They were constructed into the shapes mimicking those of the shale bings (waste heaps) that are a feature of West Lothian. They run for a distance of 1,000 feet and are sometimes home to sheep that are left to graze on the grass formations. In 2007 the sheep's owner painted them red to 'brighten things up'.

Lomondgate *Stag*

The *Stag* was designed by artist Andy Scott and unveiled in 2012. Made of welded steel, it stands 20 feet high and weighs 2 tons. Depicting a stag and its reflection in water, it is located on a roundabout at Lomondgate business park near Loch Lomond.

Arria

None of the 70,000 motorists who drive past Cumbernauld on the M80 each day will have failed to notice *Arria*. The 33-foot-high steel sculpture of a woman is also by Andy Scott. She is named after Arria Fadilla, the mother of Antoninus the Roman emperor who ordered the construction of the Roman Empire's most northerly defensive wall.

Heavy Horse

Fifteen feet high, the *Heavy Horse* by Andy Scott stands beside the M8 motorway on the eastern edge of Glasgow at Easterhouse.

LITTLE SPARTA

Artist Ian Hamilton Finlay created a garden to display over 275 artworks at his isolated home near Dunsyre in Lanarkshire. He moved there in 1967 and, due to his agoraphobia, hardly left before his death in 2006. The garden is now regarded as an artwork in itself and can be visited by the public during certain times of the year.

TURNER PRIZE SCOTS

The Turner Prize is Britain's most prestigious modern art prize. Douglas Gordon was the first Scot to win, in 1996. He had exhibited Alfred Hitchcock's film *Psycho* slowed down to run for 24 hours. In 2010 Susan Philipsz won for sound installation *Lowlands*, which was a traditional Scottish lament being sung by her and originally played under three Glasgow bridges. The following year sculptor Martin Boyce won for his installation *Do Words Have Voices*. Glasgow School of Art has produced five winners. As well as Gordon, Philipsz and Boyce, Simon Starling won in 2005, Richard Wright in 2009 and fellow alumnus Duncan Campbell won in 2014.

MUSIC

Scotland's love of music is expressed in many different forms and has reached far beyond the country's shores. In terms of instruments, the bagpipe is known and loved (and occasionally loathed) the world over. Scots who emigrated are credited as an inspiration for American folk music and the most famous rock and roll star of all time is credited with Scottish ancestry. The first Presley to reach America came from Aberdeenshire and arrived in the New World in 1745.

THE MOD
The Mod, from the word *mòd* meaning assembly, is the festival of Gaelic music and the arts. There are local mods but the Royal National Mod is the main event of the year. It lasts over a week and includes poetry as well as music and dancing competitions. A game of shinty (see page 209) is also played – the 2015 event had 3,000 competitors.

SCOTTISH COUNTRY DANCING
A part of Scottish country life, the ceilidh is a social evening which often involves storytelling, singing and dancing.

Scottish country dancing is a more formal pastime, which consists of reels, jigs, strathspeys and waltzes. Some well-known dances include:

- Dashing White Sergeant

- Eightsome Reel

- Strip the Willow

- Gay Gordons

- Reel of the Fifty-first Division

- St Bernard's Waltz

- Highland Schottische

- Canadian Barn Dance

- Kelly's Kaper

- Sausage Machine

BAGPIPES

No musical instrument has a more recognisable national association than the bagpipes. Although identifiably Scottish, musical instruments of the same type have been found in Europe, Africa and Asia. The Great Highland bagpipe is the form seen in Scotland and is composed of a chanter, a blowpipe, a bass drone, two tenor drones and, of course, the bag. The inspirational sound of the pipes has been played in battlefields from the

Western Front in the First World War to the Persian Gulf more recently. Each year the World Pipe Band Championships are held in Glasgow.

BOTHY BALLADS

These were traditional songs sung by those working on the land. They are associated with the north-east of Scotland and were named after the farm buildings where agricultural workers stayed. They originate from the middle and latter years of the nineteenth century. The poet and songwriter Hamish Henderson, who is credited as being behind the revival of interest in Scottish folk music, spent time collecting bothy ballads among other songs in the 1950s.

'DONALD, WHERE'S YER TROOSERS?'

This comic song was a hit for Scots singer Andy Stewart in 1961 and tells of the reception a young man gets when he 'comes down from the isle of Skye' wearing his kilt. Andy Stewart and other singers such as Kenneth McKellar, Moira Anderson and Peter Morrison were popular entertainers during the 1960s and 1970s.

DID YOU KNOW?

Staple of the Last Night of the Proms 'Rule, Britannia' was written by a Scot. James Thomson's eighteenth-century poem was adapted into the crowd-rousing song. Another staple of an event held in London is the hymn 'Abide with Me', which since 1927 has been sung at the English FA Cup final. It was written by Scot Henry Lyte, who was born in the Borders.

HARRY LAUDER

Lauder was a hugely popular singer and stage performer of the early twentieth century. He created a Scottish character that mixed sentimentality with a canny Scottish humour and emphasised being careful with money, which may have contributed to this perception of Scots that persists to this day. His repertoire included 'I Love a Lassie', 'A Wee Deoch-an-Doris' and 'Roamin' in the Gloamin''. Lauder wrote 'Keep Right on to the End of the Road' in tribute to his son who was killed in the First World War. He had taken an active part in the war effort: recruiting, entertaining the troops on the Western Front, and fundraising for the Million Pound Fund for Maimed Men, which led to him being knighted in 1919.

POPULAR MUSIC

Scotland has produced many well-known popular music bands and singers over the years:

Altered Images	Hue and Cry
Arab Strap	Jesus and Mary Chain
Average White Band	Lonnie Donegan
Aztec Camera	Lulu
Bay City Rollers	Nazareth
Belle and Sebastian	Orange Juice
Big Country	Paolo Nutini
Calvin Harris	Primal Scream
Camera Obscura	Simple Minds
Cocteau Twins	Teenage Fanclub
Deacon Blue	Texas
Donovan	The Associates
Eurythmics	The Proclaimers
Franz Ferdinand	The Sensational Alex Harvey Band
Glasvegas	

The Skids   Wet Wet Wet
Travis

GREAT SCOTS
THE PROCLAIMERS (1962–)

Craig and Charlie Reid have been together as The Proclaimers since the 1980s. Their blend of authentically Scottish singing voices, heartfelt lyrics and melodic tunes has seen them become one of the country's favourite live acts. Their anthemic 'I'm Gonna Be (500 Miles)' is sung at parties, weddings and football matches – and as they are supporters of Edinburgh's Hibs, their ballad 'Sunshine on Leith' is played at each home game. The twins have been politically active throughout their career and their first album featured 'Letter from America', a lament to the generations who had left their native Scotland to look for a new start in life.

'MULL OF KINTYRE'

One of Scotland's most successful songs was written by a Liverpudlian with Irish ancestry. Following his success with The Beatles, Paul McCartney had bought a farm in the Mull of Kintyre. Its isolated location inspired him to write the ballad, which featured a pipe band from nearby Campbeltown. The song was a huge hit in Britain, staying at number one in the charts for nine weeks and selling over two million copies. McCartney described it as a love song 'about how I enjoyed being there – imagining I was travelling away and wanting to get back there'.

DID YOU KNOW?

John Lennon spent many of his childhood holidays in the Highlands. The future Beatle had cousins from Scotland and they'd spend weeks in Durness. Lennon returned to Scotland in 1969 with his wife Yoko, her daughter Kyoko and his son Julian. It was not to become a happy memory as Lennon crashed the car they were in and had to spend time in hospital.

GREAT SCOT
SUSAN BOYLE (1961–)

There have been few introductions to popular fame as dramatic as Susan Boyle's. She appeared on ITV's talent show *Britain's Got Talent* on Saturday 11 April 2009, and her audition piece was 'I Dreamed a Dream' from *Les Miserables*. There were few who thought the 47-year-old who walked onto the stage and talked about her dream of being a professional singer would have the impact she did. The video on YouTube of her first appearance has over 200 million views. Her first album was a bestseller – the highest-selling debut album by any British artist – and she continues to be doing what she had dreamt.

GLASGOW BARROWLAND BALLROOM

One of the country's best-loved music venues sits in Glasgow's East End. As its name suggests, it was designed for dancing – it has a sprung floor – but as a live music venue it has earned a legendary reputation. Some of the musical acts that have played there include:

Alice Cooper, Beastie Boys, Bjork, Blondie, Blur, Bob Dylan, Calvin Harris, Cocteau Twins, Coldplay, David Bowie, Deep Purple, Dinosaur Jr, Duran Duran, Echo and the Bunnymen, Eminem, Foo Fighters, Grace Jones, Green Day, Happy Mondays, Human League, Ice T, Iggy Pop, Iron Maiden, Justin Timberlake, Katy Perry, Kraftwerk, Metallica, Moby, Morrissey, Motorhead, Muse, New Order, Oasis, Orbital, Paul Weller, Pixies, PJ Harvey, Primal Scream, Public Enemy, Pulp, Radiohead, Ramones, REM, Robbie Williams, Robert Plant, Run DMC, Sigur Rós, Siouxsie and the Banshees, Soft Cell, Sonic Youth, Stiff Little Fingers, Stone Roses, Suede, The Clash, The Jesus and Mary Chain, The Kinks, The Pogues, The Proclaimers, The Smiths, The Waterboys, The Wedding Present, U2.

DID YOU KNOW?

Elvis Presley made his only appearance on British soil in Scotland. The King was making his way back to America from military service in Germany when his plane landed at Prestwick to refuel on 3 March 1960. Fans greeted the legendary singer enthusiastically but some were disappointed he didn't remove his army cap.

TELEVISION

We're doomed!

Few portrayals of Scotsmen in television have the irascibility and crabbiness of the dour Private James Frazer in *Dad's Army*.

He was played by John Laurie, a respected cinema and stage actor before putting on the khaki of the Walmington-on-Sea Home Guard.

DID YOU KNOW?

Doctor Who graduated from a Scottish university. The Timelord has made several references in the show to gaining a medical degree from the University of Glasgow.

SCOTTISH TV SHOWS

The nation that invented television would be expected to produce some good programmes. Whether that is true or not is in the eye of the viewer, but some of the more notable programmes made in Scotland include:

Super Gran

Gudrun Ure played the grandmother superhero who was pitched against a baddie called The Scunner Campbell. Billy Connolly sang the theme tune, which included the line 'She's got more bottle than United Dairies'. The show ran in the mid-1980s for two series.

Taggart

The line 'There's been a murder' has become this long-running Glaswegian crime show's catchphrase. Detective Chief Inspector Jim Taggart was hard-bitten, cynical and tough, played by the hangdog-faced Mark McManus. When he died, the show lived on, with various actors playing the chief inspector's role. The show ran from 1983 to 2010.

Chewin' the Fat

This BBC Scotland sketch show starred Ford Kiernan, Greg Hemphill, Karen Dunbar, Mark Cox and Paul Riley. Among the many memorable characters were the Banter Boys, two middle-class gents who revel in working-class behaviour and banter; Betty, the once-promiscuous old lady who shocks care staff with tales of her amorous adventures; and the Lighthouse Keepers, who gave the world the catchphrase 'Gonnae no dae that'.

Still Game

This sitcom featured two pensioners called Jack and Victor who had been friends since childhood and retained their sense of fun while living in the Glasgow housing estate of Craiglang. The characters have appeared in a stage play of the same name and in *Chewin' the Fat*. The series was made into a live show which was performed twenty-one times at the Glasgow Hydro. It returned to TV in October 2016.

Take the High Road

This soap opera ran from 1980 to 2003 and the 1,520 episodes featured the lives of the residents of the fictional village of Glendarroch. (The Loch Lomond village of Luss was the location for exterior filming.) Hollywood star Alan Cumming appeared in the show in 1986 as an evil woodcutter.

Weir's Way

Tom Weir and his trademark Fair Isle jerseys and red bobble hat could be seen all over Scotland as he visited places the length and breadth of the country. His friendly manner and curiosity made him a much-loved broadcaster and while the show was popular from 1976 to 1987 it attained a level of cult viewing when STV later repeated it in the early hours. Pop band Aberfeldy recorded a song in tribute.

Tutti Frutti

This 1987 six-part drama was written by John Byrne and starred Emma Thompson and Robbie Coltrane. It follows the adventures of Scottish rock and roll band The Majestics on a tour of Scotland. However, when one of the band members dies before the tour kicks off, his lookalike brother (played by Robbie Coltrane) takes over.

River City

BBC Scotland had never broadcast a home-made soap opera until *River City* was first shown in 2002. It centres on a community living in the fictional Glasgow area of Shieldinch. The characters have experienced the typical soap opera events of affairs, murders, disappearances, reappearances and betrayals.

Rab C. Nesbitt

The unemployed, alcoholic Govan resident made his first appearance in sketch show *Naked Video* and got his own show in 1988. In his string vest, headband and forlorn pinstripe suit, Rab was fond of the chance to air his views on the world. His long-suffering wife was Mary Doll and his main partner in crime was his friend Jamesie Cotter.

Hamish Macbeth

There have been many police drama serials but few are set in the Scottish Highlands. Robert Carlyle played the eponymous police constable in the fictional village of Lochdubh, for which Plockton was used. Nothing too harrowing or gruesome happened in Lochdubh and Macbeth was careful not to do anything that would lead to him being promoted out of his dream job.

SHETLAND NOIR

Following the success of Nordic noir crime series, such as *The Killing* and *The Bridge*, a similar type of show was filmed in Scotland. Called *Shetland*, it featured Detective Inspector Jimmy Perez, played by Douglas Henshall, and was adapted from the crime novels of Ann Cleeves.

C. U. JIMMY

A memorable portrayal of a Scotsman, if not for all the right reasons, was that by English comic Russ Abbot. His C. U. Jimmy character had bright ginger hair, wore a green kilt and spoke in a rapid Scottish accent. A range of See You Jimmy tartan tammy hats, with ginger hair extensions out the back, are commonly worn by tourists.

RADIO

Scotland has its own dedicated BBC station: Radio Scotland, which broadcasts a mix of sport, news, and music. A Gaelic-language station is Radio nan Gàidheal and is complemented by its television station BBC Alba.

HAMISH AND DOUGAL

These two Scottish characters appear in the BBC Radio 4 comedy show *I'm Sorry I Haven't a Clue* and also in the spin-off series *You'll Have Had Your Tea*. They were played by Graeme Garden, who was Scottish, and Barry Cryer, who wasn't (being from Yorkshire).

CINEMA

Scotland does not have its own film studios, but despite this some entertaining movies have been made in the country:

GREGORY'S GIRL (1981)
This Bill Forsyth film pulled off the impossible: making Cumbernauld new town the most romantic place on earth. The film's hero Gregory struggles with his feelings of love for a fellow pupil, but with the advice of friends and a wise young sister he is eventually directed towards his girl.

LOCAL HERO (1983)
Another Bill Forsyth film, *Local Hero*, won its way into the hearts of millions of cinemagoers through its charming story of Highland locals presented with the opportunity of untold fortunes through the plans of an American oil company.

TRAINSPOTTING (1996)
The film of Irvine Welsh's 1993 book was directed by Danny Boyle. Among the cast were Ewan MacGregor and Robert Carlyle. Coupled with a contemporary soundtrack, it presented Edinburgh to the wider world in a way that had never been seen, from the first scene of shoplifters running down Princes Street. A sequel was released in 2017.

HIGHLANDER (1986)
Highlander starred Frenchman Christopher Lambert as Connor MacLeod, an immortal warrior who is trained by an Egyptian-Spanish immortal played by Sean Connery. MacLeod faces a climactic battle with his rival, in modern-day New York.

BRAVEHEART (1995)

Mel Gibson starred in and directed this biopic of the life of William Wallace. Although it's peppered with historical inaccuracies, the spirit of Wallace's struggle for independence is conveyed as well as in any other Hollywood epic.

THE WICKER MAN (1973)

This horror film about a pagan island community that welcomes a Christian policeman from the mainland investigating a missing girl was mostly filmed in Dumfries and Galloway and in Ayrshire.

ROB ROY (1995)

Hollywood visited Scottish history again the same years as *Braveheart* with the cinematic telling of Highland legend Rob Roy MacGregor. The same year that William Wallace was portrayed by a short Australian, Rob Roy was played by tall Irishman Liam Neeson.

BRIGADOON (1954)

A musical starring Gene Kelly as an American who discovers a Highland village that rises out of the mist once every 100 years and only for one day. He falls in love with a villager and faces the choice of leaving his life in New York behind for a woman he's only known for a day.

I went to Scotland and found nothing there that looks like Scotland.

ARTHUR FREED, BRIGADOON PRODUCER
(THE FILM WAS SHOT IN A STUDIO IN CALIFORNIA)

WHISKY GALORE! (1949)

The islanders of the appropriately named Todday (a hot toddy being a cold remedy involving whisky) battle to salvage as much of the whisky from a wrecked ship as they can before the authorities stop them. This much-loved Ealing Studios film was shot on Barra.

SUNSHINE ON LEITH (2013)

This feel-good musical has classic songs from The Proclaimers in a story of two young soldiers returning to their life in Edinburgh. Contains a mass singalong of 'I'm Gonna Be (500 Miles)'.

GREAT SCOT
SEAN CONNERY (1930–)

Sean Connery remains Scotland's most famous actor. Born in Edinburgh, he was a milkman before his physique saw him find work as an artist's model and helped him secure the role of James Bond. He played the laconic secret agent seven times and it made him famous worldwide. He attempted to forge a career away from the shadow of 007 and appeared in many critically acclaimed films such as *The Hill*, *The Man Who Would Be King* and *The Name of the Rose*. Connery made a memorable appearance as the eponymous hero's father in *Indiana Jones and the Last Crusade*, and also won an Oscar for his performance as an Irish cop in *The Untouchables*. In a poll to find the Top 100 Scots of the twentieth century, conducted by Scottish cultural and heritage website Scran, Sean Connery came top.

'BROADSWORD CALLING DANNY BOY'

This famous movie line comes from the 1969 war film *Where Eagles Dare* which was adapted from the novel by Alistair MacLean. Born in Glasgow, MacLean was a hugely successful thriller writer who also wrote *The Guns of Navarone* and *Ice Station Zebra*, which were turned into films too.

FICTIONAL SCOTS ON SCREEN

Montgomery 'Scotty' Scott

The engineer in the original cast of American science fiction TV show *Star Trek* was born in Linlithgow in 2222. He also spent time as an 'Aberdeen pub-crawler'. Scotty was chief engineer for the starship *Enterprise*, continuing a long line of Scottish engineers.

Groundskeeper Willie

William MacDougal works at Springfield Elementary School in long-running TV cartoon *The Simpsons*. From Kirkwall in Orkney, Willie is as stereotypically Scottish as it's possible to be, with his red hair and dour demeanour, which often leads to aggression.

James Bond

Behind the suave, sophisticated and occasionally violent British secret agent there lie Scottish roots. His father was Andrew Bond, who hailed from Glencoe. The inspiration for 007 is believed to be Fitzroy Maclean, who was a friend of Bond author Ian Fleming. Maclean operated behind enemy lines as a member of the SAS in the North African desert and then in Yugoslavia during the Second World War.

Scrooge McDuck

Donald Duck's uncle is the richest duck around. Great uncle to Huey, Dewey and Louie, he is known for his vast wealth but also his fondness for looking after his money.

Stuart Mackenzie

Stuart is the father of Charlie, a beat poet who is frightened of relationship commitment, in the Mike Myers' film *So I*

Married an Axe Murderer. Stuart memorably tells his ginger-haired son William to get his big head out of the way so he can watch television, a head he describes as 'an orange on a toothpick'. Myers has played several other Scots on screen, including Fat Bastard in the *Austin Powers* series and the lovable ogre Shrek.

COMEDY

From the nineteenth century onwards, Scots found they had more free time available as working hours decreased, so naturally they went looking for some light relief – and not just in the pub, which was seen as the preserve of the male worker.

Theatres and music halls put on variety shows with singers, dancers and other acts, and these proved to be hugely popular. While this form of entertainment has long gone, stand-up comedy remains one of the entertainment staples still treading the boards.

GREAT SCOT
BILLY CONNOLLY (1942–)

Billy Connolly started his working life in the Glasgow shipyards and then found his true vocation by appearing on stage: firstly as a folk musician and then as a solo comic. In 1975 he made his first appearance on the BBC's *Parkinson* programme, which catapulted him to national fame. Connolly – known as the Big Yin – was immediately recognisable with his long hair and beard, and his mischievous observational comedy served as an inspiration for many comics. He appeared in films, including a career high in *Mrs Brown*, where he played Queen Victoria's ghillie John Brown.

GLASGOW EMPIRE

The problem with Freud is that he never had to play the Glasgow Empire second house on a Friday night.
KEN DODD, COMEDIAN, ON ANALYSING COMEDY

The Glasgow Empire was a notorious venue for acts that were not confident or good enough. They faced immediate censure from the audience if they did not come up to the quality the punters felt they deserved. In a story, possibly apocryphal, that illustrates the hard time that could await performers, English double act Mike and Bernie Winters came up to play the venue. Mike went on first and after a few minutes his brother Bernie appeared, peeking around the curtain. At which point a voice from the stalls shouted, 'Good god, there's two of them.'

SCOTTISH JOKES

While it is easy to generalise, Scots' humour can be dry and wry. It can also be dark in tone. When Billy Connolly burst onto the scene in 1975 on *Parkinson*, it was chiefly via a joke he told involving a woman's corpse. To give an idea of the sorts of things that make Scots laugh, here are some:

What do you call a pigeon that goes to Aviemore for its holidays? A skean dhu.

'You know the Scottish boomerang? You throw it and it sings about coming back.' (Billy Connolly)

'I'm Scottish and Jewish – two racial stereotypes for the price of one.' (Arnold Brown)

A woman goes into the local newspaper to place a death notice for her husband. She writes down what she wants: 'Jim Smith, from Peterhead. Dead' and hands over her money. The newspaper clerk says to her, 'For that amount you can put more words down.' She takes back the bit of paper, thinks for a moment, writes then hands it back. It now reads, 'Jim Smith, from Peterhead. Dead. Ford Escort for sale.'

A Glaswegian goes into a bakery. He points at the cabinet and asks, 'Is that a doughnut or a meringue?'
'No, you're right, it's a doughnut.'

A tourist in Edinburgh sees a kilted bagpiper and goes up to him.
'Excuse me, I have to ask, is anything worn under the kilt?'
'No, ma'am,' he replies. 'It's all in perfect working order.'

What's the smallest town in Scotland?
Perth. It's built between two Inches
(The town has two parks: North and South Inch)

A man was walking through Glasgow's Blythswood Square when he was approached by a woman of the night. She asked him if he'd like 'super sex'. He thought for a moment then replied: 'I don't know, what kind of soup is it?'

THEATRE

In 1540, Sir David Lyndsay's *Ane Satyre of the Thrie Estaits* was first performed for King James V, but Scottish theatre as we know it today properly began in the eighteenth century with plays such as John Home's 1756 tragedy *Douglas*, which was a popular success. During one performance, an audience member was so impressed he shouted out, 'Whaur's yer Wullie Shakespeare noo?'

The Scottish Church looked on plays with a disapproving eye. Home received so much criticism from the kirk that he left Scotland to continue his craft in England. The fact he was a church minister himself only served to add fuel to the kirk's ire. One well-known playwright of the late eighteenth and early nineteenth centuries was Joanna Baillie (a church minister's daughter) who wrote twenty-seven plays as well as poetry.

The theatre continued to be constrained through Church and government censorship, but the start of the nineteenth century saw successful staging of theatrical versions of Walter Scott's novels, such as *Rob Roy*. So popular was it that a performance was organised especially for the visit of King George IV in 1822 at the Theatre Royal in Edinburgh.

It wasn't until the twentieth century that Scottish theatre was to fully make its mark, although it became dominated by English touring companies making the journey north and there was no professional theatre until the second half of the century. The Citizens Theatre in Glasgow was founded in 1943 and Edinburgh's Traverse Theatre opened in 1963. Both were to be part of a revival in the theatre in Scotland.

In the 1970s, plays reflected the keen interest in politics and explored themes such as Scottish nationalism. Among the works of the time were John McGrath's play *The Cheviot, the Stag and the Black, Black Oil*, which was first performed in 1973. It was played by the radical 7:84 company, whose name derived from the statistic that 7 per cent of the population owned 84 per cent of the country's wealth.

In the twenty-first century, the theatre in Scotland continued to enjoy good health. The National Theatre of Scotland was established in 2006 and one of its first productions was Gregory

Burke's powerful *Black Watch* about a group of Scottish soldiers who had fought in Iraq.

'THE SCOTTISH PLAY'

It is considered bad luck to refer to Shakespeare's play about Macbeth by its title and so is known by this euphemism.

DID YOU KNOW?

The world's biggest arts festival takes places every year in Edinburgh during August. The Edinburgh Festival encompasses the Fringe and the official International Festival as well as others, such as the Book Festival.

DID YOU KNOW?

Actor Alec Guinness, who is known for playing Obi-Wan Kenobi, appeared in the first Edinburgh Festival in 1947 acting in Shakespeare's *Richard II*.

FOOD AND DRINK

FOOD

Experience would seem to show that the food of the common people in Scotland is not so suitable to the human constitution as that of their neighbours of the same rank in England.
ADAM SMITH, THE WEALTH OF NATIONS (1784)

BURNS SUPPER

The idea of celebrating the life of Scotland's best loved poet with a meal – and a drink – originated in a memorial dinner held in 1801, five years after Burns' death, when a group of his friends gathered together in the cottage where he was born in Alloway. The idea grew and now Burns Suppers are held globally. They can be informal or more formal, depending on the attendees and the setting, but generally they involve the eating of haggis, along with 'neeps and tatties' (turnips and potatoes), which is accompanied by a recital of Burns' 'Address to a Haggis'. Other works are also recited and all is accompanied by the drinking of whisky.

Fair fu' your honest, sonsie face,
Great chieftain o the puddin'-race!
Aboon them a' ye tak your place,
Painch, tripe, or thairm:*
Weel are ye worthy o' a grace
As lang's my arm.

ROBERT BURNS, 'ADDRESS TO A HAGGIS' (1786)

THE SELKIRK GRACE

Some hae meat and canna eat,
And some would eat that want it;
But we hae meat, and we can eat,
Sae let the Lord be thankit.

Robert Burns is reputed to have offered these words in response to an invitation by the Earl of Selkirk. There is another unattributed form of grace, which goes:

Grace, pace round the table,
Eat as much as you are able.
When you're done, lay down your spoon
Grace, pace, Amen.

---

*   Stomach, tripe or intestines

DID YOU KNOW?

In the 1770s a new food was introduced to Scotland: the turnip. As a dessert. A visitor to the city from England, Edward Topham, said that Scots who couldn't get their hands on fruit were keen to eat anything that resembled fruit. These small turnips were eaten 'as if they had been the fruit of the first perfection'.

FOODSTUFFS FROM SCOTLAND

If an epicure could remove by a wish, in quest of sensual gratifications, wherever he had supped he would breakfast in Scotland.
SAMUEL JOHNSON, JOURNEY TO THE WESTERN ISLANDS OF SCOTLAND (1775)

Some foodstuffs are as linked with Scotland as images such as lochs, stags and castles, and others are directly associated with the country through their names. Some of the more notable include:

BREAKFAST

Porridge
Traditional porridge is made with oats, salt and water but those not able to face such a Calvinistic start to the day use a combination of full-fat milk, sugar, bananas, honey or syrup to help.

Square Sausage

Also known as Lorne (possibly after music hall entertainer Tommy Lorne), the square sausage is sausage meat pressed into a flattened shape and cut into squares.

Arbroath Smokies

This smoked haddock is one of Scotland's delicacies. Legend has it that a fisherman's cottage burned down and in the smouldering ruins some smoked fish were found. They were found to be delicious and so the delicacy was discovered.

SOUPS AND STARTERS

Scotch Broth

Scotch broth is a thick soup and contains barley, lamb, mutton or beef, onion, carrots, split peas and lentils.

Cullen Skink

Bearing the name of the Moray village where it originated, Cullen Skink (*skink* is an old Scottish word for soup, originally made from a boiled shin of beef) is a broth of smoked haddock, onions and potatoes.

Cock-a-leekie Soup

Cock-a-leekie's ingredients include chicken, leeks and rice or barley. Prunes are also added to the pot to add sweetness and colour.

BREADS

Potato Scones

Not a scone in the traditional sense but a flat bread. A 'tattie scone' perfectly accompanies a fry-up.

Well-fired Roll

To some, 'well-fired' might suggest burnt, but these bread rolls with their crusty, blackened top surfaces are a staple of Scottish bakers.

Buttery

The buttery is a savoury flat roll from the north-east, where they are also known as 'rowies'.

MAIN MEALS

Haggis

Haggis is to Scotland what the hamburger is to America. This concoction of sheep offal, beef, oatmeal, suet, onions and spices – cooked inside a sheep's stomach – is Scotland's national dish. If these ingredients are not to everyone's taste, a vegetarian version replaces the meat with vegetables, mushroom and pulses – and leaves out the sheep's stomach.

Stovies

Stovies is a dish that can result in strong discussion being exchanged as to its correct ingredients, with some declaring that the main ingredient of mashed potatoes should be accompanied by onions and mince, while others insist it should be bacon, lamb, roast beef, corned beef, square sausage, sausage, roast beef, leeks, carrots or even cabbage. A properly prepared plate of stovies should 'stick to the ribs' with its qualities of solid sustenance.

Mealie Pudding

Also known as white pudding, this sausage contains oatmeal and pork.

Chicken Tikka Masala

Glasgow chef Ali Ahmed Aslam has claimed to be the inventor of one of Britain's favourite dishes. In his Glasgow restaurant the Shish Mahal he was looking for a quick recipe, used tomato soup along with some spices, and the rest is history.

Mince and Tatties

Mince and tatties has been a staple for years. This dish of minced beef with boiled potatoes, with the addition of carrots, should provide enough sustenance to preclude any thought of pudding.

SWEETS, CAKES AND DESSERTS

Shortbread

Butter, sugar and flour (and sometimes salt) go together to make one of Scotland's most identifiable products. The main company producing shortbread is Walkers, which exports to more than eighty countries.

Black Bun

This dense, pastry-covered fruit cake is traditionally eaten at New Year. It was not enjoyed by Robert Louis Stevenson, who described it as 'a dense black substance, inimical to life'.

Selkirk Bannock

Similar to a fruitcake, the Selkirk Bannock comes from the town in the Borders bearing its name.

Dundee Cake

Dundee cakes have been baked since the 1800s, although there are claims that when Mary, Queen of Scots, voiced her dislike of cherries, a cake was produced with the trademark almonds arranged on top.

Tablet

This Scottish delicacy is a simple combination of butter, sugar and condensed milk. It is similar to fudge but is more crumbly.

Edinburgh Rock

Despite the suggestions of its name, Edinburgh rock is soft and is a souvenir of the city.

Soor Plooms

A sour, green, hard-boiled sweet.

Ecclefechan Tart

These tarts, similar to Christmas mince pies, come from the Dumfries and Galloway town.

Clootie Dumpling

As its name suggests, this fruit pudding is prepared in a household cloth (the 'cloot'). It is often served as dessert at Christmas and New Year, accompanied by custard.

Cranachan

A dessert of cream, raspberries, honey, whisky and toasted oatmeal.

Deep-fried Mars Bar

The most notorious item on offer to eat in Scotland. Taking a chocolate bar and frying it may sound like a step too far, but many chip shops will fry one for customers brave enough to put their arteries to the test. Scottish chip shops are not averse to frying foods not normally seen in a fryer: a Pizza Crunch is a pizza that has been deep-fried.

DID YOU KNOW?

The Abernethy biscuit does not come from the Perthshire village but from Dr John Abernethy, an eighteenth-century Scottish surgeon who was working in London. He suggested to a baker's shop he frequented that the taste of their plain biscuits could be improved by adding caraway seeds and sugar. The resultant delicacy was named in his honour.

MISCELLANEOUS

Forfar Bridie
Like its English counterpart the Cornish pasty, the bridie is a mixture of meat and vegetables encased in pastry.

Macaroni Pie
Combining two sets of carbohydrate-based foodstuffs, the pie has macaroni and cheese poured into a pie casing normally seen filled with mutton.

Scotch Pie
A small round pie with mutton filling.

Scotch Egg
It is not obvious why a boiled egg encased in meat and breadcrumbs is called a Scotch egg – its origins remain unclear.

Marmalade

Although not a Scottish invention, there was significant Scottish involvement in its development. Around the beginning of the nineteenth century, James Keiller of Dundee began producing marmalade which had the addition of the rind, and it was this product which came to represent the preserve.

Bovril

John Johnston was a butcher in Roslin when he came up with the idea of fluid beef: a product that became a hot, meat-flavoured drink called Bovril.

Crowdie

A Scottish cream cheese which is believed to date back to the time of the Vikings.

Oatcakes

Scotland was known as Land of Cakes in the sixteenth century due to its love of oatcakes.

Jeely Piece

A jeely piece is nothing more exotic than a slice of bread spread with fruit jelly.

DID YOU KNOW?

The macadamia nut is named after Scot John Macadam, who had emigrated to Australia in 1857. The tree bearing the nut was named after Macadam by a friend, who was the director of Melbourne's botanic gardens.

DOOKING FOR APPLES

A traditional game for Halloween in Scotland is ducking for apples in a pan of water – without using hands or kitchen utensils. Another food-related game at Halloween is trying to eat a treacle scone which is hung from a broomstick.

THE GOLDEN SPURTLE

Since 1994 the World Porridge Making Championships have been held in Carrbridge in the Highlands. The winner of the best traditional porridge (pinhead oatmeal, salt and water) takes home the Golden Spurtle (spurtle being the rod-shaped utensil used to stir the porridge). Competitors come from all over the world and 2016's winner was Bob Moore from Portland, Oregon.

Eh'll hev eh peh, en' en ingin' ane, an aw.
(I'll have a pie, and an onion one too.)
EXAMPLE OF DUNDEE DIALECT WHILE ORDERING FOOD

DRINK

Slàinte mhath
GAELIC TOAST MEANING 'GOOD HEALTH',
PRONOUNCED 'SLANCHA VAH'

Scots, like some other nations, are fond of 'taking a drink'. Robert Burns wrote of 'guid auld Scotch drink' and there are few social occasions where a swally (an alcoholic drink) is not partaken. It isn't a newly formed impression. In the 1750s there were 600 licenses issued to taverns in Edinburgh. With a population around 40,000, that's one for every sixty-five people – including children and the elderly.

There are two drinks heavily associated with Scotland: one is a soft drink and the other is not.

BARR'S IRN-BRU

This orange, sugary, carbonated drink was launched in 1901. Part of the mythology of Irn-Bru is that only a select few know the secret recipe that gives it its unique flavour. Each 330 ml can contains 34 grams of sugars – 38 per cent of an adult woman's reference intake (previously called the guideline daily amount).

Irn-Bru has regularly outsold Coca-Cola in Scotland, one of the few countries where the American beverage has not been the highest-selling soft drink. Memorable advertising campaigns have been utilised to sell the product using these straplines:

- Scotland's other national drink

- Made in Scotland from girders

- Irn-Bru gets you through

- That's phenomenal

A popular Christmas TV advert using Raymond Briggs's character the Snowman depicts a boy taken on a magical flight by the Snowman over Scottish landmarks and then being punished for not giving the children's character a drink from his can.

WHISKY

There is evidence of distilling in Scotland going as far back as 4000 BC. There are two main types of whisky: the blend and the single malt. Single malts are from one distillery, distilled from malted barley, while blended whiskies are a mix of single malt and grain whisky. Most whisky sold is blended.

Single malts are prized for their individual taste. If beauty is in the eye of the beholder, taste is in the glass of the drinker and what might be nectar to one imbiber is the equivalent of Brussels sprouts to another. Here are some of the more notable whiskies grouped by the traditional areas:

Campbeltown
Glen Scotia
Longrow
Springbank

Highland
Aberfeldy
AnCnoc
Ardmore
Balblair
Clynelish
Dalmore
Deanston
Edradour
Glen Garioch
Glencadam
Glendronach
Glenglassaugh
Glengoyne
Glenmorangie
Glenturret
Inchmurrin
Loch Lomond
Old Pulteney
Royal Lochnagar
Tomatin
Tullibardine

Island
Arran
Highland Park
Isle of Jura
Scapa
Talisker
Tobermory

Islay
Ardbeg
Bowmore
Bruichladdich
Bunnahabhain
Caol Ila
Kilchoman
Lagavulin
Laphroaig
Port Askaig
Port Ellen

Lowland
Auchentoshan
Glenkinchie

Speyside
Aberlour
Auchroisk

Aultmore	Glenfiddich
Balmenach	Glenlivet
Balvenie	Glenrothes
BenRiach	Knockando
Benrinnes	Macallan
Benromach	Miltonduff
Cardhu	Mortlach
Cragganmore	Spey
Craigellachie	Strathisla
Dailuaine	Tamdhu
Dalwhinnie	The Singleton of Dufftown
Glen Grant	Tomintoul
Glen Moray	Tormore
Glenfarclas	

HOGMANAY

An occasion marked by widespread consumption of drink is Hogmanay (New Year's Eve). Nowadays many cities and towns will put on special events such as concerts and firework displays to mark the end of one year and the beginning of another. Stonehaven puts on fireball-swinging in the main streets and Edinburgh has a giant street party in which 150,000 gather in the city centre.

A traditional, more low-key Hogmanay would see family members and friends 'first-foot' each other by visiting their homes after midnight (marked by the bells ringing out to bring in the new year). It is traditional that the first first-footer at the door is a tall, dark stranger and he carries his bottle (usually of whisky) and foodstuffs such as black bun. Although not seen as often in our days of central heating, the first footer would bring a lump of coal to heat the house.

On New Year's Day steak pie is on many menus, although alcohol is generally favoured by the brave, or those who weren't drinking the night and early morning before.

DID YOU KNOW?

Glenfiddich is the biggest-selling malt whisky in the world, with a 30 per cent share of the market. Meanwhile, Dufftown in Moray is known as the 'malt whisky capital of the world' due to the number of its distilleries. This is celebrated in an old rhyme:

Rome was built on seven hills,
Dufftown stands on seven stills.

ANGELS' SHARE

During maturation in its oak barrels, an amount of whisky is lost through evaporation. This can be up to 2 per cent each year and is known as the angels' share.

BUCKFAST TRIANGLE

This is the name given to the area enclosed by Airdrie, Coatbridge and Cumbernauld. Buckfast is a tonic wine made by the monks of Buckfast Abbey in Devon which has great appeal to younger drinkers of these areas.

BEER

Scots are no strangers to beer and one of the country's most famous is Tennent's Lager, brewed in Glasgow's east end. Craft beers have increased in popularity to stand alongside more traditional ales. Some of the beers brewed in Scotland include:

Lerwick Brewery
60° North
Skipper's Ticket
Lerwick IPA

Valhalla Brewery
Simmer Dim
Island Bere
Spring I'da Air

Oban Bay Brewery
Fair Puggled
Kilt Lifter
Skelpt Lug

Strathaven Ales
Claverhouse
Old Mortality

WEST Beer
King Tut's
St Mungo

Innis & Gunn
Toasted Oak IPA
50 Shades of Green

Belhaven
Belhaven Best
Wee Heavy
St Andrews Ale
Robert Burns Ale

Caledonian Brewery
Deuchars IPA
Flying Scotsman
Auld Lang Syne
Over the Bar

Brewdog
Punk IPA
Dead Pony Club
Nanny State

Kinneil Brew Hoose
Kincardine Sunset
Wonderfu' Jake

Stewart Brewing
Embra
Cauld Reekie
First World Problems

Broughton Ales
Old Jock Ale
Black Douglas
The Ghillie

Traquair House Brewery
Jacobite Ale
Bear Ale

Scottish Borders Brewery
Foxy Blonde
Dark Horse

Tempest Brewing Company
In the Dark We Live
Long White Cloud

Barney's Beer
Marshmellow Milk Stout
The Hanging Bat

Harviestoun Brewery
Bitter & Twisted
Schiehallion
Old Engine Oil

Williams Brothers Brewing Company
Caesar Augustus
Fraoch
Birds & Bees
March of the Penguins
Kelpie

Isle of Arran Brewery
Red Squirrel
Clyde Puffer
Arran Blonde

Ayr Brewing Company
Leezie Lundie Pale Ale
Rabbie's Porter

Fyne Ales
Highlander
Cloud Burst

Houston Brewing Company
Braveheart
Warlock
Jock Frost

Loch Lomond Brewery
Ale of Leven
Silkie Stout

Inveralmond Brewery Ltd
Ossian
Thrappledouser
Inkie Pinkie
Santa's Swallie

St Andrews Brewing Co
Fife Gold

Kelburn Brewery
Tartan Army
Goldihops
Ca' Canny

Windswept Brewing
Tornado
Typhoon

An Teallach Ale Company
Suilven
Hector

Black Isle Brewery
Hibernator Oatmeal Stout

Cairngorm Brewery
Nessie's Monster Mash

Cuillin Brewery
Pinnacle

Cromarty Brewing
Happy Chappy
Atlantic Drift

Hebridean Brewery
Berserker

Isle of Mull Brewing Company
Terror of Tobermory

Orkney Brewery
Dark Island
Skull Splitter
Clootie Dumpling

Isle of Skye Brewing Company
Young Pretender
Lord of the Ales

Swannay Brewery
Orkney Blast

SCOTS PINT
Before the introduction of imperial measures in the nineteenth century, a Scots pint was the equivalent of three imperial pints.

DRUNK
Just as Eskimos are supposed to have many words for snow, Scots have many words for being drunk:

blazing
blootered
fou' (full)
gone
guttered
half-cut

hammered
merracked
peeshed
steam-boats
steaming
stocious

SPORT

Sport is important to Scots, perhaps too much at times, as it can affect the nation's psyche. It is thought part of the reason Scotland didn't vote for devolution in 1979 is the poor showing of the national football team in the World Cup the previous year. Scots have excelled in a number of sports and although disappointment can be close to hand, a number of sports now and then produce moments of magic.

FOOTBALL

Football is Scotland's national sport, bringing pain, sorrow and joy (not in equal measure) to fans of the game. The late Victorian period saw an increase in leisure time for thousands of workers and football served as an ideal outlet with games played on Saturday afternoons, fitting in when the workers had finished for the week. The Scottish Football Association was formed in 1873 and remains the game's chief authority in Scotland. Scots didn't invent football but are credited with coming up with the passing game, which was in contrast to the dribbling style of English teams.

Scots played an important part in the early game in England. Several English teams played with most of their players being 'Scotch professors' (so named as it was felt the Scottish game was more scientific than the English one at the time) and the English Football League was founded in 1888 by William McGregor, from Perthshire. The first professional footballer was James Lang when he signed for Sheffield Wednesday in 1876.

England was not the only country to feel Scottish influence in its game's development. Scots helped establish football in countries such as Czechoslovakia, Uruguay, Argentina and Brazil. It was little consolation to Scottish fans to know that when Brazil beat their team in the World Cup finals of 1982, 1990 and 1998 it was a Scot, Archie McLean, who had introduced the passing game to the country.

The King forbiddis that na man play at the fut ball under the payne of iiij d.
ACT OF PARLIAMENT, 1424, DURING REIGN OF KING JAMES I. THOSE WHO DEFIED THE BAN WERE FINED THE PRINCELY SUM OF FOUR PENCE

Another attempt to ban football (and golf) took place in 1457 when James II wished his subjects to participate in more military-minded pursuits, i.e. archery.

DID YOU KNOW?

Berwick Rangers play in the Scottish leagues, despite being part of England since 1482.

36-0

For many years the world's highest-scoring game was a match in 1885 when Arbroath beat Bon Accord 36–0. Bizarrely, the very same day, another game on the east coast had a similar score. Dundee Harp beat Aberdeen Rovers 35–0, or it could have been 37–0. The officials lost count and erred on the side of caution. In 2002 a match in Madagascar had a score of 149–0 but this was a thrown game.

GREAT SCOTS
BUSBY, STEIN, SHANKLY AND FERGUSON

Some people believe football is a matter of life and death.
I can assure them it is much more important than that.
BILL SHANKLY

Matt Busby (1909–94), Jock Stein (1922–85) and Bill Shankly (1913–81) all worked in coal mines before becoming footballers, and then managers for Manchester United, Celtic and Liverpool respectively. Busby led his team to European Cup victory in 1968, after the Munich Air disaster ten years before when his 'Busby Babes' team lost eight players. The European Cup was first won by a British side in 1967 by Jock Stein's Celtic, who won every tournament they entered that season and would win nine leagues in a row. He was known as the 'Big Man' for his stature and the way he dominated the game in Scotland. He died of a heart attack after guiding Scotland to the 1986 World Cup finals.

After Celtic's victory in Lisbon, Stein was congratulated by a Scottish manager who said to him, 'John, you're immortal now.' That man was Bill Shankly, who attained a level of immortality himself by resurrecting Liverpool, taking them to the top of the English First Division in 1964, and winning the FA Cup in 1965 and the UEFA Cup in 1973.

Liverpool's rivals along the M62 were Manchester United, who in 1986 saw another Scot take over. Alex Ferguson (1941–) had taken Aberdeen to the highest level, winning three Scottish leagues and the European Cup Winners' Cup in 1983, beating Real Madrid. He struggled at first at Old Trafford but in 1999 he realised a dream for the club when they beat Bayern Munich in the dying minutes to lift the European Champions League Cup, the first win in Europe's top competition since 1968. The irascible Scot retired in 2013 after having guided Man United to thirteen league titles, five FA cups, two European Champions Leagues and one European Cup Winners' Cup.

DID YOU KNOW?

The first all-seater stadium in Britain was in Clydebank. Kilbowie Stadium had seats installed in 1977.

STATUES AND MEMORIALS TO SCOTTISH FOOTBALLERS

Bill Shankly	Glenbuck, Ayrshire
Bill Shankly	Anfield, Liverpool
Jim Baxter	Hill o' Beath, Fife
Matt Busby	Old Trafford, Manchester
Denis Law	Old Trafford, Manchester
Alex Ferguson	Old Trafford, Manchester
Dave Mackay	Pride Park, Derby
Denis Law	Aberdeen Sports Village, Aberdeen
Davie Cooper	Hamilton Palace Sports Grounds, Hamilton

Billy Bremner	Elland Road, Leeds
Jimmy Johnstone	Celtic Park, Glasgow
Jock Stein	Celtic Park, Glasgow
Billy McNeill	Celtic Park, Glasgow
John Greig	Ibrox Park, Glasgow

GREAT SCOTTISH SPORTING MOMENTS: CELTIC WIN THE EUROPEAN CUP

Jock Stein had taken over Celtic in 1965. The following year they won the Scottish League and so qualified for the European Cup. With a team of talents, such as Jimmy Johnstone, Bobby Murdoch, Bobby Lennox, and led by captain Billy McNeill, they progressed to the final, which was played in Lisbon on 25 May 1967 against Inter Milan. Celtic went a goal behind and were then forced to attack the defensively minded Italians. Their fluent passing game saw the Scots go 2–1 ahead and claim the trophy. Celtic were the first northern European club to lift the cup.

Showing the strength of Scottish football in this one year, a week later Rangers were finalists in the Cup Winners' Cup final, losing to Bayern Munich 1–0. (The Scottish club would take home the trophy five years later after beating Dynamo Moscow.) Scotland had beaten current World Cup champions England in April, a game that saw Rangers' Jim Baxter so confident of not being caught in possession that he toyed with the English team by playing keepy-uppy with the ball on Wembley's hallowed turf.

DID YOU KNOW?

Dumfries' football team Queen of the South is the only Scottish team whose name is in the Bible, in Luke 11:31.

They'll be dancing in the streets of Raith tonight.

FOOTBALLING RECORDS

Scotland's national stadium, Hampden Park, was the world's biggest football ground until 1950. Games played there hold several world records:

YEAR	TEAMS	MATCH	ATTENDANCE
1937	Celtic v Aberdeen	Scottish Cup final	147,365
1937	Scotland v England	Home international	149,415
1960	Real Madrid v Eintracht Frankfurt	European Cup final	127,621
1970	Celtic v Leeds United	European Cup semi-final	136,505

GREAT SCOTTISH SPORTING MOMENTS: ARCHIE GEMMILL SCORES AGAINST HOLLAND

In 1978 Scotland had travelled to the World Cup in Argentina full of hope. They lost 3–1 to Peru and then drew with Iran. The last game required Scotland to win by three clear goals to get past Holland and qualify for the second stage. The Scots started badly, going a goal down before taking control and scoring three: the last being one of the greatest goals scored at the World Cup. Archie Gemmill received the ball outside the box and started towards the goal, taking the ball past one defender then another and then a third before curving his shot beyond the Dutch keeper. TV commentator David Coleman said Scotland were now 'in dreamland' and he was right. Minutes later the Dutch scored and Scotland were exiting dreamland.

DID YOU KNOW?

The only football ground in Europe to have a hedge as part of its infrastructure is in Scotland. The hedge at Brechin City's Glebe Park runs half the length of the pitch.

BA' GAMES

A number of towns in Scotland play a rugged form of football far from the regulated system seen in the professional leagues. The games take place between two teams from the same town, with participants playing for the side that represents the part of town they live in. The games are won when the ball reaches a specific area. In Jedburgh the uppies have to get the ball over the wall at Jedburgh Castle, while their opponents, the doonies, attempt to get it across the Skiprunning Burn. There is no football, as such, but much grabbing and tussling, and shops along the route show their preparedness by having their windows boarded up. Towns that have had ba' games include Jedburgh, Hawick, Kirkwall, Cockburnspath, Denholm, Scone and Duns.

MOTORSPORT

Scotland has produced two great world champions of the motorsport world. They raced on different surfaces: Jim Clark on the track and Colin McRae on the gravel, asphalt, mud and snow of the world rally circuit. Described by *Autosport* as perhaps 'the greatest natural talent ever seen in Formula 1' Clark won the Formula 1 World Championship in 1963 and then again two years later and only lost in 1962 and 1964 due to mechanical problems. In a Formula 2 race on 7 April 1968 at Hockenheimring his car came off the track and hit nearby trees, killing the Scot instantly.

Colin McRae was born into rallying, his father Jimmy having been British champion. Colin showed a committed and flamboyant driving style that at times cost him points, but in 1995 in a Subaru Impreza he won the World Rallying Championship – Britain's first-ever winner. Always a keen competitor he was unable to reach the heights of 1995 again, although his drives for Subaru and later Citroen helped them secure the constructor's championships. He died in a helicopter crash in 2007.

Other notable Scots racers include Jackie Stewart, who won the World Drivers' Championship three times and campaigned for better safety for the F1 drivers. More recently David Coulthard raced with McLaren and came second in the Drivers' Championship in 2001.

BOXING

Scots have long had a reputation for being battlers, either with themselves, foreign armies or people who inadvertently spill your pint. With a reputation for having fighting qualities, it is no surprise that Scotland has produced several world champion boxers, including recent champions Alex Arthur (world super-featherweight champion) in 2007 and Ricky Burns (WBA super-lightweight) in 2016.

GREAT SCOT
BENNY LYNCH (1913–46)

*I felt I was fighting for Scotland and any true happiness
lies in the fact that I did not let Scotland down.*
BENNY LYNCH, 9 SEPTEMBER 1935

The Glaswegian Lynch became Scottish flyweight champion in 1934 and the following year, on 9 September, the 5-foot-3-inch-tall 'wee man' from Glasgow became world champion, the fight against Jackie Brown being stopped by the referee after two rounds. He defended his title three times, appearing in front of large crowds in the open air at football grounds. In 1938 he was stripped of his title due to being overweight. Lynch was an alcoholic and died aged only thirty-three.

THE FIGHTING CARPENTER
Ken Buchanan was given this nickname as he'd practised the trade before boxing professionally. Buchanan won 61 out of his 69 fights, one of which made him world lightweight champion in 1970. He is regarded as one of Britain's best-ever boxers.

ATHLETICS

The Scottish word *stechie* means someone without any apparent athletic prowess. It does not apply to the following who became Olympic champions.

GREAT SCOTTISH SPORTING MOMENTS: ERIC LIDDELL WINS OLYMPIC GOLD

The secret of my success over the 400 metres is that I run the first 200 metres as hard as I can. Then, for the second 200 metres, with God's help, I run harder.

ERIC LIDDELL

Eric Liddell was born in China to Scottish missionaries in 1902. He studied at the University of Edinburgh, where, as well as running in the athletics club, he played rugby, winning seven caps for Scotland.

In the Paris Olympic Games of 1924, Liddell was due to run in the 100 metres but withdrew when he discovered the heats were on a Sunday: as a committed Christian he wouldn't compete on the Sabbath. He also did not take part in the relay events for the same reason. He chose to run in the 200- and 400-metre events and in the 200-metre final he took the bronze medal. Two days later it was the 400-metre final. He powered ahead and ran the first 200 metres in a time thought to be too fast to be maintained: 22.2 seconds. The Scot showed no sign of fatigue and crossed the finishing line to create a new world record.

Liddell became a missionary in China but was interned in a Japanese camp and died in 1945. The Eric Liddell Centre is based in Edinburgh's Morningside area and provides specialist caring services for the local community.

GREAT SCOTTISH SPORTING MOMENTS: ALLAN WELLS WINS THE OLYMPIC 100 METRES

The build-up to the 1980 Olympics, held in Moscow, saw pressure exerted by Margaret Thatcher for British athletes to boycott against the USSR's military involvement in Afghanistan. Going into the games, Edinburgh's Allan Wells was Commonwealth

200-metre champion. In Moscow, Wells progressed smoothly through the qualifying rounds. His chief rival in the final was Silvio Leonard from Cuba whom he was level with through the latter part of the race. Just before the line, Wells dipped. It was enough to give him the gold. It was the first Scottish win on an Olympic track since Eric Liddell. Some felt that his victory was devalued because countries including the USA had boycotted the games. Two weeks after the Olympics, Wells raced the two top Americans at a meeting in Koblenz. He won.

RUGBY

Rugby was keenly played in the Borders, and the area provided several players who took part in one of the game's most exciting matches in 1990.

GREAT SCOTTISH SPORTING MOMENTS: SCOTLAND WIN THE GRAND SLAM

When England came to Murrayfield on 17 March 1990 there was all to play for. In that year's Five Nations Championship both teams had won their previous three games, but England were expecting to win easily. Fans arriving in Edinburgh were seen wearing T-shirts proudly sporting the words 'England – Grand Slam Winners'. The winner of the match would secure not only the Grand Slam, but also the championship, the Triple Crown and the Calcutta Cup.

Before kick-off, Scottish captain David Sole led his team out in a slow walk that was designed to get the crowd firmly behind the team. The Murrayfield crowd had other reasons to cheer as Scotland went ahead with two penalties before England came back with a try to make it 6–4. Scotland then scored another penalty to go 9–4 ahead at half-time. Soon after the restart,

Scotland's Gavin Hastings kicked the ball forward before being bundled off the pitch. The ball bounced and was caught by the chasing Tony Stanger, who touched down for the try. England scored a penalty to make it 13–7 and then put the Scots' defence under pressure, but the home side hung on for a famous victory.

DID YOU KNOW?

The Calcutta Cup was once severely dented after players from the Scotland and England rugby teams went on a night out with the trophy in Edinburgh's pubs following a match in 1988.

TENNIS

Scotland was not known as a tennis-playing nation, but all that changed when a young man from Dunblane burst onto the world stage.

GREAT SCOT
ANDY MURRAY (1987–)

Andy Murray showed great talent when he made his debut in the senior game in 2005. He developed his stamina and mental strength to go with his playing ability and the rewards came with a victory in the US Open in 2012 – the first British player to win a Grand Slam event since 1977. A year later he made history by defeating Novak Djokovic at Wimbledon, making Murray the first British male singles champion for 77 years. Continuing his run of successes, he won Wimbledon again in 2016 and played a major part in not only restoring Britain to the top division of the Davis Cup, but in them winning the event in 2015. In November 2016 he became the men's ATP world number one.

GOLF

Scotland is the home of golf. The oldest course in the world is Musselburgh Links in East Lothian and the Fife seaside town of St Andrews is the location for the R&A, which governs the worldwide game (with the exception of the USA and Mexico) and the most famous golf course in the world: the Old Course. The Old Course features the iconic Swilken Bridge, seven double greens, and the infamous seventeenth 'Road Hole', with its blind tee. Winners of the Open Championship when held at St Andrews include:

Tiger Woods (2000, 2005)   Bobby Locke (1957)
John Daly (1995)   Sam Snead (1946)
Zach Johnson (2015)   Peter Thomson (1955)
Nick Faldo (1990)   Bobby Jones (1927)
Seve Ballesteros (1979, 1984)   James Braid (1905, 1910)
Jack Nicklaus (1970, 1978)

DID YOU KNOW?

The first Open Championship was played in Scotland, at Prestwick, in 1860. The Ayrshire course hosted the first eleven tournaments but hasn't featured on the roster since 1925.

SHINTY

Similar to the Irish game of hurling, shinty is mainly played in the Highlands and Outer Hebrides. The Camanachd Cup is the most prestigious competition, which began in 1896 with a Kingussie win. The Badenoch side won twenty league titles in a row up until 2005, a feat which was recognised by Guinness World Records.

CURLING

The sport of curling requires freezing weather if played outdoors – in milder winters it has relied on the use of indoor ice rinks. Evidence of the 'roaring game' (so named due to the players' cries and noise of the stones on the ice) goes back as far as the sixteenth century and the curling club in Kilsyth dates back to the early eighteenth century. In the 2002 Winter Olympics, Britain won gold in the women's team event, the first Winter gold since Torvill and Dean in 1984. All team members were Scottish.

SNOOKER

With many towns in Scotland having their own snooker halls, it is no surprise the country has produced some of the game's finest players. Walter Donaldson won the World Championship in 1947 and then three years later, but two players at the end of the twentieth century and into the twenty-first dominated the tournament:

Stephen Hendry   1990, 1992, 1993, 1994, 1995, 1996, 1999
John Higgins   1998, 2007, 2009, 2011

Graeme Dott also won in 2006.

CYCLING

It is appropriate that the country that gave the world the pneumatic bicycle tyre has also provided several world-class cyclists. One is Graeme Obree, who broke the world hour record in 1993 on a bike, 'Old Faithful', which contained a part of a washing machine. He broke the record again in 1994. Chris Hoy became Britain's most successful Olympian at the 2012 Olympics when he won his sixth gold medal. Another great Scot on the saddle is Mark Beaumont, who set a new record in cycling around the world when in 2008 he completed the long-distance trek in 194 days, 17 hours.

HIGHLAND GAMES

Around eighty Highland Games are held in Scotland during the summer. The most southerly is at Peebles in the Borders. Tradition has it that clan chiefs would run games in order to select the fittest and strongest of their clans for future battles. A Highland Games will host several different sports which include:

TOSSING THE CABER

The caber is a tree trunk cut and shaped to size (usually about 19 feet long and weighing 150 pounds) that has to be lifted on the shoulder. The competitor then runs, stops, and launches the caber so that it turns end over end and lands as close as possible to the 12 o'clock position. It is not about achieving distance.

PUTTING THE STONE

This game is similar to the shot-put, as seen in track and field events. There are two types of play: the first is with the Braemar stone (up to 26 pounds in weight) which has no run-up to the launching of the stone and the other is with the open stone (up to 22 pounds) which can involve a run-up.

THROWING THE HAMMER

Originally the hammer was that of the local blacksmith, but when used in sporting events the head should be spherical in shape and made of metal, with the wooden shaft being 4 feet long. The furthest distance thrown wins the event.

WEIGHT OVER THE BAR

The weight is 56 pounds and is held by a metal ring. Competitors have three attempts to throw the weight over a bar set at a specific height, using only one hand. A good throw means it clears the bar and lands away from the thrower; a bad throw can result in a speedy exit from the throwing position due to the weight succumbing to gravity.

TUG OF WAR

Two teams compete in the traditional way.

TRACK RUNNING

Various running events are held over distances such as 100 yards, 220 yards and 1 mile.

HILL RACE

A local hill is chosen for this event and the race starts and ends inside the arena.

It is a rule of the Scottish Highland Games Association that all competitors in the heavy events must wear kilts, and they must not get dressed or undressed in the arena.

Competitions in bagpipe music and dancing also take place. Among these is the famous Highland Fling. The Cowal Games in Dunoon is the biggest, with 3,500 competitors.

DID YOU KNOW?

The founder of the modern Olympic Games, Frenchman Pierre de Coubertin, introduced the hammer throw and shot-put into the games after seeing an exhibition in Paris in 1889 of the Highland Games. The tug of war was also included but withdrawn in 1920.

MYTHS AND LEGENDS

Scotland has more than its share of myths and legends and some continue to fall under the adage: 'When the legend becomes fact, print the legend.' They fly in the face of that hoary old chestnut called 'fact', but Scotland would be a duller place without their mystery. Some concern the very symbols of the nation itself.

THE SALTIRE

Scotland's flag is a white cross on a light blue background. It is also known as St Andrew's Cross as it represents the story of Scotland's patron saint being crucified on a X-shaped cross. Legend has it that the flag was originated when a white cross appeared in the sky before a ninth-century battle, in what is now East Lothian, between the Picts and Scots under Angus mac Fergus against the Angles led by Aethelstan. Angus took this to be an omen and when he was then victorious the cross was adopted as Scotland's flag. There is a Flag Heritage Centre in the East Lothian village of Athelstaneford.

THISTLE

Scotland's national flower is the thistle, although the reasons behind the choice are lost. Legend has it that a band of Scots soldiers was resting at night when an enemy was creeping up on them. These enemy troops (possibly Vikings) walked into a patch of unseen thistles and their cries of pain alerted the Scots, who were able to mount a successful defence. Whatever the reason, there is a deep appropriateness: the rich beauty of the purple flower, attached to the sharp end of the spines.

UNICORN

Although it is fictional, the unicorn is Scotland's official animal. During the reign of King James III a design of a unicorn wearing a crown was introduced as a royal emblem and a gold coin was also brought in that was called the unicorn. It is thought that the mythical beast was chosen, as its natural enemy was the lion – the symbol of England.

DID YOU KNOW?

Pontius Pilate is rumoured to have been born in Scotland. The Roman who presided over the trial of Jesus is claimed to have been the son of a Scottish woman and a visiting Roman official. The story fails on one fact though: the Romans did not arrive in Scotland until decades after Jesus' death.

SUPERNATURAL BEINGS

Scotland's long, dark nights of winter are the perfect breeding ground for tales of the supernatural. The citizens had plenty of opportunity to gather round the fireside and exchange stories of the scary and the sinister. While many stem from centuries past, there is still the occasional sighting that causes the hairs on the back of the neck to rise.

One type of mysterious being is a benshie (the equivalent of the Irish banshee). These female spirits would foretell a death in the family with their wailing cries. Some Highland families have similar entities: the Macleans of Lochbuie were said to be visited by a ghost of an ancestor riding a spectral horse around the house. This type of phantom is known as a bodach.

Being a country with numerous islands and a long coastline, it is not surprising that some of the supernatural beings inhabit water. The Blue Men of the Minch (the area of water between the Scottish mainland and the Outer Hebrides) are reputed to emerge from their undersea caves to attack sailors. One account describes them wearing blue caps and having 'grey faces which appear above the waves'. A traditional fisherman's song includes this verse:

*And if my boat be storm-toss'd and beating for
the bay,
They'll be howling and be growling as they
drench it with the spray;
For they'd like to heel it over to their laughter
when it lists,
Or crack the keel between them, or stave it with
their fists.*

Another creature to emerge from the depths is the boobrie, a beast that may take the form of a very large bird, a water bull or a water horse. They are said to be as big as seventeen eagles.

One of the most well-known aquatic beings is the selkie, which is a seal able to shed its skin and become human. The MacCodrums of North Uist are said to be descended from a male human and a female seal, who had taken human form. Another well-known sea creature is the mermaid, of which there have been several reported in Scotland at Benbecula, Galloway, Knockdolian Castle, Port Glasgow, the River Dee and Sandwood Bay.

A legend of the Scottish mountains is that of the Big Grey Man, a mysterious figure on the slopes of the Cairngorms' highest mountain: Ben Macdui. It was in 1925 that an account of an encounter with this supernatural being was given, by Professor Norman Collie, an experienced mountain climber. At a meeting of the Cairngorm Club in Aberdeen in December 1925, Collie recounted being on the mountain's summit when he heard footsteps behind him. He couldn't see anything in the mist to suggest the source. Suddenly he was 'seized with terror' and started running off the hill in a blind panic. He vowed not to return to Ben Macdui on his own.

There were various theories about what Professor Collie had encountered, whether it was a Yeti-like creature, or his own footsteps echoing back from the rocks. Other supposed encounters with the Big Grey Man have been put down to a phenomenon called the Brocken Spectre, which occurs when certain lighting conditions cause a person's shadow to be multiplied in size and projected onto clouds, thus giving the idea of a separate, larger-scaled being close by.

Not as big as the Big Grey Man but probably more useful around the house was the domestic sprite known as a brownie. They would cheerfully help out with household duties, and also assist bringing in the harvest, but if the family to which the brownie was attached tried to reward him, it would become upset and vanish. These creatures gave their name to a junior branch of the Girl Guides who are encouraged to help with domestic duties.

THE FAIRY FLAG

A story has long been told about the clan chief of the MacLeods of Dunvegan in Skye. He is said to have married a fairy who gave him a flag, which she promised would bring good fortune to his clan – as long as it was only used three times. The flag has been used twice, at battles in 1490 and 1580, at which the MacLeods were victorious. Although tattered, the flag is still in existence and can be seen in Dunvegan Castle.

AULD NICK

Chief among the supernatural beings is the Devil, who has acquired many nicknames over the centuries:

Auld Nick	Black Donald
Auld Hornie	Earl o' Hell
Auld Clootie	Thrummy Cap
Auld Roughie	Lucky Piper
Bad Man	Uncle Geordie

SAWNEY BEANE

Sawney Beane is Scotland's most notorious cannibal, a depraved leader of an incestuous gang in Ayrshire who feasted on anyone passing their den. He was then hunted by the king's forces and executed. Or at least that's what the myth says. Despite his name being often aired, there is no documentary evidence of Beane's existence, crimes or punishment. The dates given of him being active range from the thirteenth to the sixteenth century, which suggests he is more fable than fact.

GHOSTS

Many in Scotland have a good ghost story in them and many spirits are said to haunt Scottish locations. Castles are a favourite venue.

BALGONIE CASTLE
This Fife castle is said to be haunted by a mysterious figure known as Green Jeanie, who appears at night in certain parts of the castle.

CASTLE OF MEY
A former holiday residence of the Queen Mother, this is also the home to another green lady, supposedly of the Sinclair family. She was said to be in love with a worker on the estate and fell out of a window while trying to catch sight of her beau.

CAWDOR CASTLE
A handless ghost of a young woman is reputed to be seen here. It is said that her hands were cut off by her enraged father, the Earl of Cawdor, when he found her with a young suitor.

DUNTRUNE CASTLE
Duntrune Castle near Crinan in Argyll is the location for a story from the seventeenth century. A bagpiper loyal to clan chief Colla MacDonald alerted his leader to imminent ambush by playing a newly composed pibroch on his pipes. The warning worked and the clan chief escaped, but the piper was not so fortunate. He was punished and his hands were cut off; he subsequently died. In the nineteenth century it was said that workmen at the castle uncovered a skeleton which was missing its hands. The pibroch, 'The Piper's Warning to his Master', is still played and the ghost of the piper is claimed to haunt the castle walls.

GLAMIS CASTLE

Glamis Castle is host to several ghosts, including that of Lady Janet Douglas, who was burned as a witch in 1537. Another is that of nobleman 'Earl Beardie', Alexander Lindsay, the fourth Earl of Crawford, who refused to stop playing cards on the Sabbath and ended up playing cards with Auld Nick himself. He lost and the Devil took his soul and condemned him to play until Doomsday. It is said that the earl can still be heard enjoying a game.

HERMITAGE CASTLE

Mary, Queen of Scots, is said to haunt this castle. She made a dramatic 20-mile horse ride from Jedburgh to visit the fourth Earl of Bothwell (whom she later married) who was recovering from a stab wound. On her way back she fell ill and later said, 'Would that I had died in Jedburgh.'

TANTALLON CASTLE

In 2009 a photograph was published showing what appeared to be a ghostly figure standing at a window in the ruins of the East Lothian castle. The figure, possibly of a woman in sixteenth-century dress, was photographed by a castle visitor.

THE MONTROSE GHOST

One of the most well-known ghosts in Scotland is that of a pilot. Montrose was the home to two squadrons of the Royal Flying Corps and in May 1913 a tragic accident resulted in the death of Lieutenant Desmond Arthur. In the years afterwards a strange figure was seen at the base. It was only after an enquiry that cleared the pilot of any wrongdoing that the ghost was no longer sighted.

THE BRAHAN SEER

Known in Gaelic as Coinneach Odhar, the sixteenth-century Brahan Seer was first written about in the nineteenth century.

He is said to have made predictions but as they were recorded after the events concerned it is hard to be sure of their veracity. One of them was:

> *Oh Drumossie, thy bleak moor shall, ere many generations have passed, be stained with the best blood of the Highlands.*

Drumossie, outside Inverness, is where the battle of Culloden was fought in 1746.

Another figure who was claimed to have powers of prophecy was the thirteenth-century Thomas the Rhymer, from near Melrose in the Borders. 'True Thomas' is supposed to have predicted the Battle of Flodden and the Union of the Crowns. He is said to have gained his powers of prediction after being taken away by the Queen of Elfland.

ROBERT THE BRUCE'S SPIDER

One of the greatest myths of Scottish history is that while Robert the Bruce was in hiding, he was forced to lay up in a cave. As he contemplated giving up his struggle against the English, his mind was turned by watching a spider try, try and try again to build a web. The story, while illustrative of Bruce's determination, stems from the pen of Walter Scott, who wrote of it in *Tales of a Grandfather*. It may well have an early and authentic origin, but if so it has been lost in the mists of time.

THE CURSE OF SCOTLAND

The ace of spades is associated with death but in Scotland another card has connotations beyond its place in the deck as the nine of diamonds. It is known as 'the curse of Scotland'. The origins of this label are unclear but some suggest it stems from the Battle of Culloden in 1746. It is claimed that before the battle the Duke of Cumberland wrote orders on a nine of diamonds, but there are mentions of it as the curse before the battle. Some sources suggest that it is due to the similarity of the card to the coat of arms of the Earl of Stair, who authorised the Glencoe Massacre in 1692.

GREAT SCOT
ROB ROY (1671-1734)

In the pantheon of Scottish legendary heroes and heroines there is always a place for Rob Roy MacGregor. He was a cattle dealer who was declared bankrupt in 1712 and subsequently lost his lands. Raibert Rudah (Robert the Red, because of his red hair) dallied with the Jacobite uprisings of 1715 but was also supplying the government side with information. MacGregor became an outlaw but was eventually pardoned in 1725 and died in 1734. Regarded as a Robin Hood-like legendary figure during his lifetime – he famously left a receipt after raiding a grain store – his reputation was enhanced greatly by Walter Scott's eponymous novel of 1817.

MYSTERIES OF SCOTLAND

These three are among the many unsolved mysteries of Scottish history:

WHY DID RUDOLF HESS FLY TO SCOTLAND?
On the night of 10 May 1941, a lone figure parachuted to the ground south of Glasgow. He said his name was Albert Horn and that he needed to speak to the Duke of Hamilton, whose Dungavel House was just over 10 miles away. It soon became apparent that he was Rudolf Hess, Adolf Hitler's deputy. The

Duke of Hamilton, a serving RAF officer, who had spent time in Germany before the war, went to speak with Hess and then reported to Prime Minister Winston Churchill. Hess spent the rest of his life in prison, and from the 1960s was the only prisoner in Berlin's Spandau Prison. He died in 1987, aged ninety-three, after hanging himself.

Why had this senior Nazi flown 900 miles, alone, at night, from Germany to Scotland? He claimed he was there to end Britain's involvement in the war. Had Hitler approved his plan? Hess said he hadn't, and when news of the flight was made public Hitler denounced him as being deranged, but this was seen by some as merely a cover. There are even claims that the man wasn't even the real Hess. It is believed that some files on the case have gone missing from British archives and the truth may never be known for certain.

WHAT HAPPENED TO THE FLANNAN ISLES LIGHTHOUSE KEEPERS?

The Flannan Isles lighthouse off the Outer Hebrides was completed in 1899. The following year the lighthouse was to become known for one of Scotland's most enduring mysteries. The lighthouse crew of three men – James Ducat, Thomas Marshall and Donald McArthur – were due to be visited by a relief ship on 26 December. When the boat *Hesperus* arrived, a search of the lighthouse and island found no sign of the men. Two sets of the men's oilskins were missing and a chair was overturned. Robert Muirhead, the superintendent who reported to the lighthouse board, reasoned that the men had gone out of the lighthouse and then down to the landing and had been swept away by a wave. Despite this, other explanations were touted. Had two of the men been murdered by a crew member who then killed himself by jumping into the sea? Had a sea serpent attacked them? Aliens? Were they kidnapped by foreign agents?

Ghostly voices were said to be heard on the island. Had they been literally spirited away? Whatever the fanciful reasons put forward, three men had died.

WHAT WAS SEEN IN THE DECHMONT WOODS?

On the morning of 9 November 1979 a forestry worker named Bob Taylor took his dog for a walk in the woods at Dechmont, near Livingston. When he arrived back at his house his wife was shocked by his appearance: his clothes were dirty and ripped and he had a scratch on his face. He claimed he had been attacked by small spheres which were attempting to take him towards a 'flying dome' that he'd seen hovering over a clearing.

As Taylor had graze marks on his body, the police recorded what they thought was an assault. When Taylor took them to the site, there were unexplained marks on the ground at the clearing. One of the detectives investigating the incident said:

> *We must accept the story of Mr Taylor. He is a very highly respected member of the community and a man of high integrity and not one likely to invent such a story.*

Various explanations were offered such as Taylor being confused by the planet Venus or that he had suffered a fit. He died in 2007 and maintained his experience was as described, saying, 'I know what I saw.' The location of the incident is not far from Bonnybridge, near to Falkirk, which gained much attention in the 1990s after a spate of UFO sightings.

WHAT IS THE LOCH NESS MONSTER?

Loch Ness is home to the greatest of all Scottish myths and legends: a mythical creature, for which thousands of holidaymakers arrive each year hoping to catch a glimpse. The first reports of Nessie stem from the time of Columba. The monster was attempting to attack a swimmer when Columba formed the sign of the cross in the air and said, 'Thou shalt go no further, nor touch the man; go back with all speed.' The monster speedily withdrew. Over the years there have many other sightings, photographs taken and film footage recorded. Scientific expeditions using marine technology have been used, but so far no definite evidence has been produced to prove that Nessie exists. Possible explanations for Nessie include the following:

1. Seal
2. Killer whale
3. School of porpoises
4. Plesiosaurus
5. Large newt
6. Eel
7. Sea serpent
8. Elephant
9. Greenland shark
10. Submerged trees

BUILDINGS AND STRUCTURES

Scotland's built environment serves as a useful reminder of its history and innovation whether it's ancient castles or recent additions such as the Falkirk Wheel.

CASTLES

Castles first appeared as the Norman influence spread into Scotland. The feudal system of governance meant these stone buildings represented a nobleman's power over his subordinates. Of Scotland's hundreds of castles over the centuries, many remain in existence.

EDINBURGH CASTLE

> *A sad and solitary place, without greenery and by reason of its vicinity to the sea, unwholesome.*
> QUEEN MARGARET, WIFE OF KING ALEXANDER III, IN A
> LETTER TO HER FATHER, ENGLAND'S KING HENRY III

Edinburgh's castle is one of the most famous landmarks in Scotland. With its great advantages of height and difficulty of unwelcome access, it is not surprising that its location on Castle Rock has seen human habitation at least as far back as 900 BC. In AD 600 the men of the Gododdin tribe were recorded leaving the 'fortress of Eidyn' to fight a battle thought to be at Catterick in Yorkshire. By the eleventh century, it was of major importance to Scotland's monarchs and the castle has played a pivotal role in Scottish history throughout the following centuries.

St Margaret's Chapel

The oldest part of the castle – and indeed the city – was built around 1130 by King David I in tribute to his mother, Queen Margaret. Twice a week fresh flowers are brought to the chapel by the St Margaret's Chapel Guild, membership of which is restricted to women whose name is Margaret.

Royal Palace

The palace was the home for the later Stewart monarchs, although it fell out of use, replaced by the more comfortable and spacious accommodation at Holyrood. James VI was born in the palace in 1566.

Great Hall

Built in the early sixteenth century and used for banqueting and ceremonial occasions, it was later used as a barracks and then a hospital.

Mons Meg

This large medieval cannon (or 'bombard') was a gift to James II by France's Duke of Burgundy in 1457. Its name originates from where it was tested in Europe. Weighing over 5 tons and designed to fire cannon balls 20 inches in diameter, it was used in anger at several sieges but was retired from service in 1550. The giant weapon was used once more after its retirement in 1558 when it was fired as part of the celebrations marking the marriage of Mary, Queen of Scots, to the French Dauphin. Showing Meg's power, the gun stone travelled a distance of almost 2 miles.

Prison
The castle has held Scottish prisoners from the Jacobite uprisings, French prisoners from the Seven Years War and Napoleonic Wars, American captives taken during the American War of Independence, and in 1939 shot-down Luftwaffe airmen were taken to the castle following a raid on the naval yards at Rosyth in Fife.

Esplanade
Each summer the esplanade is the venue for the military tattoo and music concerts.

Half Moon Battery
The curved, eastwards-looking section of the castle that sits above the entrance gates.

National War Museum
Part of the National Museums of Scotland, the museum tells of the military history of Scotland through displays of weapons, uniforms and other artefacts.

Scottish National War Memorial
It was opened in 1927 and contains the names of every Scottish serviceman or woman, or others who have served in a Scottish regiment, who have died in all conflicts since the First World War.

DID YOU KNOW?

A swastika can be seen inside the memorial. The symbol is featured on the cloak of a figure in one of the stained-glass panels. The swastika had been used as a symbol for good fortune for centuries and in 1927 did not have the connotations that it would gain following the rise of Nazism. Swastikas can be seen on several other war memorials, including at Balmoral Castle.

One o'Clock Gun

The gun is fired each weekday and Saturday at 1 p.m. exactly. The tradition started in 1861 as a time signal to ships in the Firth of Forth. It is silent on Christmas Day and Good Friday and during the First World War it was requested the gun be left unfired due to its startling effect on troops suffering from shell shock who were convalescing in the city. This request was granted.

Dog Cemetery

A small corner of the castle is used to bury the dogs of the garrison's officers and also regimental mascots.

Crown Jewels

The crown jewels (officially the Honours of Scotland) are kept in a secure room. They were hidden after the 1707 Act of Union and lay untouched for over a century until discovered by Walter Scott.

Sceptre	Given to James IV in 1494 by Pope Alexander VI.
Crown	First worn in its present form at Mary of Guise's coronation in 1540. The early version of the crown had been worn by James IV in 1503 at his marriage to Margaret Tudor. It was subsequently used in the coronations of Mary, Queen of Scots, James VI, Charles I and Charles II.
Sword of State	A gift of Pope Julius II to James IV in 1507. The sword was damaged during its removal in 1651 to prevent it falling into the hands of Oliver Cromwell.

The extreme solemnity of opening sealed doors
of oak and iron, and finally breaking open a
chest which had been shut since 7th March 1707,
about a hundred and eleven years, gave a sort
of interest to our researches, which I can hardly
express to you, and it would be very difficult to
describe the intense eagerness with which we
watched the rising of the lid of the chest.
WALTER SCOTT WRITING TO J. W. CROKER, 5 FEBRUARY 1818

In 1818 Walter Scott, along with senior officials of Scotland, was given permission to enter the Crown Room – a strong room in the castle where it was thought the Honours had been kept since 1707 – and determine their existence and condition. An oak chest was broken open and the Honours were found inside. They were later placed on public view and visitors were charged a shilling for entry.

The Stone of Destiny

The Stone of Destiny (also known as the Stone of Scone) was used at the coronation of Scottish monarchs for 400 years until Edward I removed it from Scotland as a spoil of war in 1296. The Stone was then used in Westminster Abbey for seven centuries until, in 1996, it was returned to Scotland.

STIRLING CASTLE

Like its counterpart in Edinburgh, Stirling Castle sits high on a volcanic rock. Its position near to a crossing of the Forth made it important strategically and as a result the castle was subjected to many sieges, and was part of an arrangement that led to the Battle of Bannockburn. The keeper of the castle, Philip Mowbray, agreed that it would be turned over to the Scottish forces under Robert the Bruce if it was not relieved by an English army before 24 June 1314. In the end the castle wasn't relieved and Mowbray was as good as his word.

In the fifteenth and sixteenth centuries it was a major royal residence, with King James IV and James V ordering building works. Mary, Queen of Scots, was crowned in the castle's chapel and her son James VI was brought up in the castle, where he was kept away from his mother's supporters. The castle has been used as a royal residence, a prison, and an army barracks before its current role as a major visitor attraction. In 2015 it was visited by almost half a million people.

War Wolf

For the 1304 Great Siege of Stirling Castle, Edward I had ordered an advanced siege weapon called the War Wolf. The siege ended (the garrison were starving) before the giant trebuchet could be used in anger, but Edward insisted on it being fired anyway.

DID YOU KNOW?

Stirling Castle was witness to an early attempt at human aviation. In 1507 the Italian John Damian de Falcuis flung himself off the battlements to prove to King James IV that he could fly. As expected, the 'Birdman of Stirling' plummeted to the ground, landing in a dung heap. He suffered a blow to his pride and a broken leg.

DUNOTTAR

Dunottar is one of Scotland's most recognisable castles, standing proud on a red-rocked peninsular on the Aberdeenshire coast, 160 feet above the North Sea. The castle was associated with many of Scotland's most famous historic figures and events, but perhaps the most momentous was in 1651 when the Honours of Scotland were hidden at Dunottar to prevent them falling into the hands of Oliver Cromwell. Cromwell besieged the castle for eight months until its eventual surrender in 1652, but the siege was in vain as the Honours were gone. They were either smuggled out by two local women or lowered onto the beach and hidden under seaweed. They were then secured away in the local church at Kinneff.

DID YOU KNOW?

Mel Gibson's 1990 *Hamlet* movie was filmed at Dunottar.

URQUHART CASTLE

Urquhart Castle is one of the most photographed castles in the country, sitting as it does on the banks of Loch Ness. The castle was built in the 1200s and later that century it was subjected to a battering from the siege engines of Edward I. It was to change owners many times during the following centuries before becoming the ruin it is today. It was near to the castle that a colour photograph of Nessie was taken in 1977 and the lure of the adjacent loch's mysterious resident helps contribute to the castle's enchanting power: it is the third most visited castle in Scotland.

CAERLAVEROCK CASTLE

Caerlaverock's distinctive triangular shape is unique in Scotland. This moated castle occupies an important location near the Solway Firth and as a result suffered damage in various conflicts through the centuries, until it was abandoned in the seventeenth century following damage sustained during the period of the Covenanters.

KILCHURN CASTLE

Kilchurn Castle retains a commanding position at the head of Loch Awe in Argyll. The English poet William Wordsworth described it as 'wild, yet stately' and wrote a poem about the castle and its surroundings. It was built in the fifteenth century as the headquarters of the Campbells of Glenorchy and remained so for a century and a half before the clan chief moved to Perthshire. The castle became a garrison in 1689.

DID YOU KNOW?

Kilchurn and Loch Awe featured in works by artists J. M. W. Turner and Horatio McCulloch.

TANTALLON CASTLE

And, sudden, close before them showed
His towers, Tantallon vast;
Broad, massive, high, and stretching far,
And held impregnable in war,
On a projecting rock they rose,
And round three sides the ocean flows.
The fourth did battled walls enclose,
And double mound and fosse. *

WALTER SCOTT, MARMION (1808)

East Lothian's Tantallon Castle is an impressive surviving example of the curtain-wall castle design, despite only one side remaining intact. It was built on a promontory, several miles east of North Berwick, overlooking the home of thousands of seabirds: the Bass Rock.

The castle was built in the fourteenth century and was home to the family known as the Red Douglases. Often in opposition to the monarch of the day, the castle was besieged by two kings: James IV and James V. It was abandoned following the damaging siege by Oliver Cromwell's troops in 1651.

EILEEN DONAN

The small isle in the confluence of Loch Alsh, Loch Duich and Loch Long was inhabited by Irish Saint Donan in the seventh century, hence the name 'island of Donan'. A castle on the site was built by Alexander II but was reduced to rubble when the Royal Navy put down a Jacobite uprising in 1719. The castle was built anew in 1932 and there are very few tourists who

---

*   moat

come to or from the Kyle of Lochalsh who do not stop to take a photograph.

GLAMIS CASTLE

Glamis Castle, near to Forfar in Angus, has seen many additions and changes since its beginnings in the fifteenth century. It was the childhood home of the present-day Queen's mother, Queen Elizabeth the Queen Mother.

LOCH LEVEN CASTLE

This island castle is forever associated with Mary, Queen of Scots, who was imprisoned there for almost a year before escaping in May 1568. She was forced to abdicate while at the castle.

DID YOU KNOW?

The 1975 comedy film *Monty Python and the Holy Grail* used two Scottish castles: Doune Castle near Stirling and Castle Stalker in Argyll. The exchange between King Arthur, and his knights of the round table, and some taunting French troops was filmed at Doune.

DRACULA'S LAIR

The inspiration for Count Dracula's Transylvanian castle is said to be that of Aberdeenshire's Slains Castle. Author Bram Stoker stayed for a while in nearby Cruden Bay while creating his Gothic horror novel.

SKIBO CASTLE

In December 2000, the world's media descended on the Highlands. It wasn't a confirmed sighting of Nessie or an actual appearance of Brigadoon, but a wedding, of pop star Madonna and English film director Guy Ritchie. It was held at Skibo Castle, which had been owned by Andrew Carnegie.

PALACES

As well as Holyrood, Scotland has some notable royal palaces. Falkland Palace in Fife contains a corridor collection of Flemish tapestries and the oldest tennis court in the world, which was used by Mary, Queen of Scots. She was born in Linlithgow Palace, which is now a ruin but retains enough of its structure to suggest its former grandeur, in its commanding position above Linlithgow Loch.

COUNTRY HOUSES

Scotland contains a number of country houses, many of which are open to the public. They include:

Abbotsford House	Borders
Arniston House	Midlothian
Callendar House	Falkirk
Dalkeith Palace	Midlothian
Duff House	Aberdeenshire
Dumfries House	Ayrshire
Floors Castle	Roxburghshire
Gosford House	East Lothian
Haddo House	Aberdeenshire

Hopetoun House	West Lothian
House of Dun	Angus
House of the Binns	West Lothian
Manderston House	Borders
Mellerstain House	Borders
Melville Castle	Midlothian
Mount Stuart	Argyll and Bute
Paxton House	Borders
Traquair House	Borders
Wedderburn Castle	Borders
Winton House	East Lothian

ABBOTSFORD TREASURES

As a man steeped in history, Walter Scott accumulated many treasures, some of which are on show in his home at Abbotsford. They include:

- Crucifix of Mary, Queen of Scots

- Napoleon's blotter and pen case

- Lock of Nelson's hair

- Lock of Bonnie Prince Charlie's hair

- Flora MacDonald's pocket book

- Musket ball from Culloden

THE ADAM FAMILY

William Adam was Scotland's most notable architect in the first part of the eighteenth century. He designed numerous country houses such as Floors Castle, Hopetoun House and Duff House.

When he died in 1748 it wasn't the end of the Adam influence on Scottish architecture. He had three sons, John, Robert and James, who were also architects. The buildings they worked on in Scotland include Dumfries House, University of Edinburgh Old College, and Wedderburn Castle.

THE BEAR GATES
These gates at Traquair House, featuring stone bears holding the family crest, have been locked since 1745 and are not to be opened until a Stewart sits on the throne.

THE PINEAPPLE
One of the most unusual buildings in Scotland is the Pineapple near Airth. It was built in 1761 for the Earl of Dunmore and is a folly, set in a walled garden. Its carved stonework was designed to drain rainwater so that no damage is caused through frost.

ABBEYS AND CHURCHES

SWEETHEART ABBEY
Sweetheart Abbey in Dumfries and Galloway was founded by Dervorguilla, wife of Baron John de Balliol (father of the future Scottish king) in 1273. Following her husband's death in 1268 she was said to carry his embalmed heart with her at all times.

DID YOU KNOW?

Oxford's Balliol College was created by funds provided by John de Balliol as a penance, following a dispute with the Bishop of Durham in 1260.

BORDERS ABBEYS

The Borders region was home to some of the best examples of medieval abbeys, established by King David I. Unfortunately, many suffered damage during King Henry VIII's Rough Wooing in the sixteenth century.

ABBEY	FOUNDED	DETAILS
Kelso	1128	Located next to the town of Kelso, little remains of this once impressive building.
Melrose	1136	Robert the Bruce's heart is buried in the grounds at Melrose.
Jedburgh	1138	Jedburgh's abbey is the most complete of its contemporaries despite its many attacks through the centuries until the Reformation provided the final blow.
Dryburgh	1150	Set in a tranquil spot near the River Tweed, Dryburgh was sacked in 1322 by King Edward II and then in 1544 by King Henry VIII's forces. Walter Scott and Field Marshal Haig are buried in the grounds.

ROSLIN CHAPEL

Roslin Chapel was brought to worldwide recognition by the Dan Brown novel *The Da Vinci Code*, which was made into a film starring Tom Hanks.

The chapel, located just outside Edinburgh, was founded by the St Clair family in 1446. It fell into a state of disrepair and in 1842 Queen Victoria visited the site and stated that it should be restored. Work was duly carried out.

Inside, it is densely packed with decorative features that mark it out from other Scottish churches. There are many representations of the Green Man – one of the most intriguing is the depiction of crops found in America, which had not been visited by Christopher Columbus at the time of the chapel's completion. The Apprentice Pillar was supposedly built by a stonemason's apprentice who was not thought capable of creating such a design by his master. On finding the work, he killed his talented trainee through jealousy.

ITALIAN CHAPEL

Orkney is rightly renowned for its ancient sites but one more recently built is just as interesting. During the Second World War, Italian prisoners-of-war were brought to work on the Churchill barriers, built to prevent Axis submarines from encroaching on the Royal Navy ships based in Scapa Flow. Requiring a place of worship, they constructed the Italian Chapel, set in a modest building based on two converted Nissen huts on Lamb Holm.

ROUND TOWERS

Seen in many parts of Ireland, there are only two round towers in Scotland: one at Brechin in Angus and the other at Abernethy in Perthshire. Both date back a thousand years. Brechin's is 106 feet high, with its door set 6 feet above ground level to prevent easy access to intruders, while Abernethy's tower is 76 feet high and lacks the hexagonal cap of its Angus counterpart.

LIGHTHOUSES

The story of lighthouses in Scotland is dominated by one family, whose legacy can still be seen. The Lighthouse Stevensons built most of Scotland's lighthouses over a period of a century and a half.

Robert Stevenson was a civil engineer, born in Glasgow in 1772. He worked for Thomas Smith, who had an interest in improving the safety of vessels through better illumination. Smith had been appointed engineer of the new Northern Lighthouse Board in 1787 and went on to install over a dozen new or improved lighthouses, before Stevenson took over in 1808.

Stevenson gained great credit for the building of a lighthouse on the Bell Rock. This presented great difficulties as the rock was submerged 12 feet each high tide and was situated 11 miles out to sea off Arbroath.

He had three sons who all became lighthouse engineers: Alan, David and Thomas. Alan was behind the elegant 156-foot-high Skerryvore lighthouse and David built on one of Britain's most northerly islands: Muckle Flugga. Thomas's most notable lighthouse was Dubh Artach.

None of Alan's children joined the family firm but David's sons David, Alan and Charles built on the Bass Rock and created Scotland's most remote lighthouse at Sule Skerry – 40 miles west of Orkney.

Thomas's son, Robert Louis Stevenson, did not follow his father into engineering, but became a writer and one of Scotland's great literary figures. He wrote:

Whenever I smell salt water I know I am not far from one of the works of my ancestors. The Bell Rock stands monument for my grandfather; the Skerry Vohr for my Uncle Alan, and when the lights come out at sundown along the shores of Scotland, I am proud to think they burn more brightly for the genius of my father.

ROBERT LOUIS STEVENSON, MEMOIRS OF HIMSELF (UNPUBLISHED)

CANALS

The Industrial Revolution required means and ways of transportation. Railways and shipping were heavily utilised and an internal route for moving the raw and finished materials via water was required. Canals were dug to facilitate this, and while some were not financial successes at the time, they live on as tourist attractions.

CANAL	OPENED	DETAILS
Forth and Clyde Canal	1790	As its name suggests, it links the Forth to the Clyde. It is 35 miles long and allowed sea-going ships to avoid having to sail through the rough waters of Cape Wrath and the Pentland Firth.

CANAL	OPENED	DETAILS
Crinan Canal	1801	Described as 'Britain's most beautiful shortcut', the Crinan Canal runs between Ardrishaig on Loch Gilp and Crinan. Its 9 miles allows travel to the Inner Hebrides from the River Clyde without having to go past the Mull of Kintyre.
Caledonian Canal	1822	Designed by Thomas Telford, it runs 60 miles from Inverness in the north to near Fort William in the south. The building helped alleviate unemployment in the Highlands.
Union Canal	1822	The Union was designed to take coal to Edinburgh from Falkirk through a link to the Forth and Clyde.

DID YOU KNOW?

Part of the Caledonian Canal is called Neptune's Staircase and is the longest staircase lock in Britain. Its eight locks raise boats 62 feet along its quarter-mile length.

THE FALKIRK WHEEL

The Falkirk Wheel is the only rotating boat lift in the world. It was opened in 2002, and links the Union and Forth and Clyde Canals. Boats are lifted and lowered 79 feet.

SCIENCE AND TECHNOLOGY

*Of all the small nations of this earth,
perhaps only the ancient Greeks surpass the
Scots in their contribution to mankind.*
WINSTON CHURCHILL

INVENTIONS

Scotland is renowned for its inventions and discoveries. Some of them include:

1614	Logarithms	John Napier
1694	Bank of England	William Paterson
1725	Circulating library	Allan Ramsay
1748	Artificial refrigeration	William Cullen
1753	Citrus fruit cure for scurvy	James Lind
1754	'Fixed air' (carbon dioxide)	Joseph Black

1761	Latent heat	Joseph Black
1765	Steam-engine condenser	James Watt
1768	*Encyclopædia Britannica*	William Smellie (editor)
1775	S-trap toilet system	Alexander Cummings
1777	Grand piano	John Broadwood, Robert Stodart (with Dutchman Americus Backers)
1786	Parabolic lighthouse reflector lamp	Thomas Smith
1788	Steam-powered ship	William Symington
1810	Savings bank	Henry Duncan
1812	Operational passenger steamship *Comet*	Henry Bell
1816	Kaleidoscope	David Brewster
1820	Macadam road surface material	John McAdam
1823	Waterproof raincoat	Charles Macintosh
1825	Tinned salmon	John Moir
1828	Hot-blast furnace	James Neilson
1839	Adhesive postage stamp	James Chalmers
1839	Pedal bicycle	Kirkpatrick MacMillan
1839	Steam hammer	James Nasmyth

1840	Electric clock	Alexander Bain
1842	Electric railway locomotive	Robert Davidson
1842	Horse-drawn lawn mower	Alexander Shanks
1843	Fax machine	Alexander Bain
1843	Hypnosis	James Braid
1847	Chloroform	James Y. Simpson
1848	Kelvin temperature scale	William Thomson (Lord Kelvin)
1850	Paraffin	James Young
1853	Hypodermic syringe	Alexander Wood
1859	*Chambers's Encyclopaedia*	W. & R. Chambers
1861	Colour photography	James Clerk Maxwell
1864	Maxwell's equations (electromagnetism)	James Clerk Maxwell
1867	Antiseptic surgery procedures	Joseph Lister
1876	Telephone	Alexander Graham Bell
1876	24-hour clock and time zones	Sandford Fleming
1880	Fingerprint identification	Henry Faulds
1889	Inflatable rubber tyre	John Boyd Dunlop

1892	Vacuum flask	James Dewar
1893	Electric toaster	Alan MacMasters
1912	Particle cloud chamber	Charles Wilson
1922	Insulin	James Macleod
1926	Television	John Logie Baird
1928	Penicillin	Alexander Fleming
1935	Radar detection	Robert Watson-Watt
1947	Disposable nappy	Valerie Hunter Gordon
1958	Diagnostic ultrasound	Ian Donald
1964	Beta-blockers	James Black
1964	Higgs boson	Peter Higgs
1966	Automated telling machine	James Goodfellow
1996	Animal cloning	Roslin Institute
2013	Tractor beams	St Andrews University

MY SCOTLAND

PROFESSOR HUGH PENNINGTON

Emeritus Professor of Bacteriology,
University of Aberdeen

What three words describe Scottish people?

Whisky-loving (but with Buckfast lurking); Anglophobic; Divided (e.g. Nationalists v. Unionists, Central Belt v. the rest, Edinburgh v. Glasgow, Protestant v. Catholic, etc. etc.)

What is your favourite place in Scotland and why?

Aberdeen – high-quality granite architecture; entrepreneurial, unsentimental and well-organised citizens; great ancient university; close to the sea and the country.

What do you miss most about Scotland when away?

Cool summers and cool winters.

What is Scotland's greatest scientific achievement?

James Clerk Maxwell. Einstein characterised his work as the 'Maxwellian program'. Newton,

Maxwell and Einstein were the founders of modern physics. Professor at Marischal College, Aberdeen, he was made redundant when it fused with King's College, went to London after he had unsuccessfully applied for a Chair at Edinburgh, then developed the Cavendish Laboratory at Cambridge.

Which figure from Scotland's past would you most like to speak to, and what would you ask them?

I would ask Sir Robert Moray to rise from his grave in Westminster Abbey and comment on Scottish politics today. From Perthshire, he joined a Scottish regiment in the French army, was highly regarded by Cardinal Richelieu, advised King Charles I and King Charles II, engaged in a Scottish rising in the Highlands in 1653, ruled Scotland with Charles II and Lauderdale, and had wide scientific interests. He worked in a laboratory in Whitehall that was visited by Samuel Pepys ('saw a great many chymical glasses and things but understood none of them'), and is remembered today as one of the most important founders, in 1660, of the Royal Society, one of the world's premier scientific institutions.

GREAT SCOT
JAMES WATT (1736–1819)

Watt was born in Greenock and was the son of a shipbuilder. He began his career manufacturing instruments for the University of Glasgow. In 1765, while strolling on Glasgow Green, he came up with the idea of making steam engines more efficient, through the addition of a condenser. It took several years until his theories became functioning reality, and in partnership with Matthew Boulton the Watt engine was perfected by 1790. Watt's engine was a major factor in the Industrial Revolution, for example, in powering water pumps in Cornish mines and in cotton mills around the country. Industrial plants no longer needed to rely on water power and so could be built away from rivers, thus creating the industrial landscape that dominated large areas of Britain. The unit of power was named in his honour.

DID YOU KNOW?

The phrase 'Shanks' pony' is thought to have stemmed from Arbroath engineer Alexander Shanks' lawn mower, which was patented in 1842. It was the first of its kind to both cut and roll grass, and required the groundskeeper to walk with the horse-drawn machine.

GREAT SCOT
JAMES HUTTON (1726-97)

With respect to human observation this world
has neither a beginning nor an end.
JAMES HUTTON, 1785

Hutton is regarded as the founder of modern geology. In 1785, he gave a paper to the Royal Society of Edinburgh concerning the 'System of the Earth its Duration and Stability'. He had travelled around the country making observations and devised a theory that the earth underwent a process of continual change and that its formation had taken place over long periods of time. His theories faced opposition, some of it on religious grounds as a definite date of creation had been set as 4004 BC, but Hutton was later proved correct.

DID YOU KNOW?

The first political assassination by firearm took place in Scotland, in 1570, when James Hamilton shot the first Earl of Moray in Linlithgow. Moray was Regent of Scotland after his half-sister Mary, Queen of Scots, had abdicated. Hamilton was a supporter of the exiled queen.

PINKERTON'S

In 1850, the private detective agency was founded in America by Glaswegian Allan Pinkerton, who had been Chicago's first police detective. Pinkerton's agency foiled an assassination plot against President Abraham Lincoln in 1861 and Pinkerton commanded the Union Intelligence Service which became the US Secret Service. The agency was hired by Andrew Carnegie during a labour dispute at his Homestead steel plant in 1892 that resulted in the deaths of nine workers.

GREAT SCOT
THOMAS TELFORD (1757–1834)

Telford was born in Eskdale in Dumfriesshire. He began his working life as a stonemason, in England, where he developed his skills in architecture. In 1793 he started working as an engineer on the Ellesmere Canal, which included the 1,000-foot-long Pontcysyllte Aqueduct. In Scotland, he was behind the Caledonian Canal's design. In his lifetime, he worked on thirty-three canals in Britain and was responsible for over a thousand miles of roads in the Highlands (as a result he gained the nickname the Colossus of Roads).

Telford was also involved in bridge design, including the Dean Bridge in Edinburgh and Menai Suspension Bridge in Wales, and he contributed to work on churches, railways, harbours, fens drainage, reservoirs and water supply. He is buried in Westminster Abbey.

FROM STRONTIAN TO STRATOFORTRESS
In 1790, at the small Highland village of Strontian in Lochaber, an important discovery was made. An element was found which was given the name strontium. It was a soft metal and its compound strontium hydroxide was used in the extraction of sugar from sugar beet. Strontium carbonate was used in fireworks to produce the colour red. While strontium is not radioactive, its isotope strontium 90 is, and the element made up part of the atomic bombs that were carried by B-29 Stratofortress bombers

to their targets at Hiroshima and Nagasaki in 1945. With a half-life of twenty-nine years, it has long-term effects on health.

GREAT SCOT
ALEXANDER GRAHAM BELL (1847–1922)

Mr Watson, come here. I want to see you.
ALEXANDER GRAHAM BELL TO HIS ASSISTANT, THOMAS WATSON, ON 10 MARCH 1876. THESE WERE THE FIRST WORDS EVER SPOKEN ON THE TELEPHONE

Alexander Graham Bell was born in Edinburgh in 1847. He emigrated to Canada in 1870 but it was in the USA that he made his name. He had grown up in a family interested in helping those suffering from deafness: his mother had impaired hearing and his father had developed a method of communication called Visible Speech. Alexander became professor of vocal physiology at Boston University in 1873 and was interested in the practical application of converting sound into electrical signals in order to help the deaf.

The first practical phone call was made in 1876 and crucially, for Bell's future prosperity, he patented his device and formed the Bell Telephone Company. By 1886 more than 150,000 American households had the telephone installed. When he died in 1922 the telephone network of America was turned off for 1 minute in tribute to its founder. Among his many other interests, Bell was involved in the setting up of the National Geographic Society.

THE HOLLOW MOUNTAIN
Loch Awe's Ben Cruachan was given the name the Hollow Mountain due to a power station that was created inside.

Completed in 1965, it uses hydropower, taking water from a reservoir down 1,299 feet. When the electricity is not needed by the National Grid, a reversible pump-storage system pumps water back up to the reservoir, where it can be reused.

GREAT SCOT
ROBERT WATSON-WATT (1892–1973)

The Battle of Britain was mainly fought in the skies over southeast England, but there was a secret to the British victory that the Germans were not aware of until years later: radar. The detection by radio waves of aircraft, and crucially the plotting of their height and location, was a key factor in the victory. This system of detection was devised by Robert Watson-Watt from Brechin. The network of radar stations and communications was called the Dowding System, after Scot Air Chief Marshal Hugh Dowding, who was in charge.

TRANSPORT

With a large landmass and dispersed population, transport is vitally important to Scotland. A mountainous country does not lend itself to easy movement, and sea routes were used before adequate roads and then railways were built over the centuries.

ROADS

WADE'S ROADS

General Wade was the commanding officer in Scotland of the British Army from 1724 to 1740. As well as the military bases at Forts William, Augustus and George, he built roads and bridges, which were designed to facilitate speedy troop deployment. Two hundred and forty miles of roads were constructed and included routes from Dunkeld and Fort William to Inverness.

The establishment of the motor car led to roads becoming the primary routes for transport. There are currently 27,830 miles of road in Scotland.

REST AND BE THANKFUL

This stretch of the A83 road, leading up Glen Croe in the Arrochar Alps, was given its name after a stone was placed there inviting travellers to do that very thing.

A1

Generally following the route of the old Great North Road, the A1 begins at the east end of Edinburgh's Princes Street and heads through the city, then East Lothian, before turning south towards England. In places it becomes a motorway (A1(M)) during its route to London. It is Britain's longest road, at 410 miles.

ELECTRIC BRAE

The Electric Brae is an unusual feature of the A719 between Culzean and Ayr. It is the place where vehicles supposedly roll uphill against gravity via electrical forces. The real explanation is that it is an optical illusion causing the driver to think the ground is rising in front of them when it is actually falling.

A939 – COCK BRIDGE TO TOMINTOUL

This stretch of road in the Cairngorms is a traditional sign of winter as when bad weather makes its first appearance the snow gates are put in place and the road is closed. Its exposed position – 2,000 feet altitude and 20 per cent gradient – means it is susceptible to being closed when snow falls and ice forms. Ironically, the Lecht Ski Centre is situated on the road.

HIGHEST ROAD

The Cairnwell Pass on the A93 between Braemar and the Spittal of Glenshee is the highest road in Scotland, reaching an altitude of 2,198 feet.

DID YOU KNOW?

In 1763 a stagecoach journey between Edinburgh and London could take sixteen days. Twenty years later this had been reduced to four.

RAILWAYS

Scotland's first intercity line, from Glasgow to Edinburgh, opened in 1842. Within half a century most towns in Scotland were connected by rail, although the Beeching cuts of the 1960s did away with some of its rural infrastructure. Despite this, there are 2,754 miles of track in Scotland and passenger numbers continue to rise. One of the most scenic routes is the West Highland line, which has two branches, running from Glasgow to Oban or Mallaig.

TAY RAIL BRIDGE

The Tay Rail Bridge was completed in 1878. Designed by Thomas Bouch, it was the longest bridge in the world at 2 miles in length. On the night of 28 December 1879, a storm was blowing as the train from Wormit to Dundee began making the crossing. It didn't reach its destination, as the train fell into the water. All seventy-five on board were killed. It remains one of the worst railway disasters in Britain. There is still debate as to what caused the accident but the gale-force winds (10–11 on the Beaufort scale) were blowing at right angles onto the spans that collapsed.

Bouch was working on designs for the Forth Railway Bridge, but this work was given to other engineers, including John Fowler, who before the disaster had refused to allow his family to cross the Tay on the rail bridge.

The locomotive was recovered from the Tay and put back into service, where it was nicknamed The Diver.

Bouch was held primarily responsible for the disaster and he died less than a year after the collapse. The new bridge was completed in 1887 and is still in use today.

Dundee poet William McGonagall wrote of the disaster although his well-meant verse is unintentionally comic:

> *Beautiful Railway Bridge of the Silv'ry Tay!*
> *Alas! I am very sorry to say*
> *That ninety lives have been taken away*
> *On the last Sabbath day of 1879,*
> *Which will be remember'd for a very long time.*
> 'THE TAY BRIDGE DISASTER' (1880)

THE FORTH BRIDGE

The Forth Bridge's cantilever design is one of Scotland's most iconic sights. This pinnacle of Victorian engineering was the first all-steel bridge to be built in Britain and has been in use since its opening in 1890. Construction took seven years and an estimated sixty-three workers were killed. When finished, it was the longest such structure in the world at 1.5 miles long. *The Times* described it as 'the greatest engineering work of modern times'.

In 2002, the bridge was completely repainted, the first time this had been done. It was a commonly held myth that workers would start painting at one end and by the time they'd finished it was time to start again.

CAIRNGORM FUNICULAR RAILWAY

This is Britain's highest railway line. The track runs for 6,500 feet and rises 1,516 feet up Cairn Gorm mountain, taking passengers to the Ptarmigan Restaurant, which is Britain's highest, at 3,600 feet. Walkers are not permitted to use the funicular to help them reach the summit.

GLASGOW UNDERGROUND

Glasgow is the only city in Scotland with an underground railway. It is nicknamed the Clockwork Orange because the trains are painted orange.

FLYING SCOTSMAN

Perhaps the most famous train in Britain, the *Flying Scotsman* was operated by London and North Eastern Railway between London and Edinburgh. It was built in 1923 and retired forty years later. This A1-class steam locomotive was the first to go faster than 100 mph.

DID YOU KNOW?

One of Britain's most isolated train stations is Corrour, on Rannoch Moor in the Highlands. It can't be reached by public road, the nearest of which ends 10 miles away.

TRAMS

Four of Scotland's cities operated trams until they were removed from service in the middle of the last century, with one city reintroducing them in the twenty-first century.

EDINBURGH

Horse-drawn trams began in Edinburgh in 1871, but were replaced with cable-operated services in 1888 – the horses found it challenging to pull laden carriages up Edinburgh's many hills. Leith operated a different system, so passengers travelling from the city would have to transfer at the boundary called the Pilrig Muddle.

Electric trams took over in the 1920s but buses and cars spelled the end and the last tram ran in November 1956 with an estimated crowd of 100,000 watching the historic event.

In 2014 trams were reintroduced to the capital, at a cost of £776 million (plus interest), which was double the earmarked figure. The project was three years late and the planned route was curtailed with trams not reaching their proposed end point at Granton.

GLASGOW

Trams were introduced in 1872 and electric power was brought in before the end of the century. Soon trams were carrying almost 200 million passengers a year over 100 miles of track. After the First World War, the network expanded and trams reached as far as Airdrie, Clydebank and Paisley. In the 1930s the Coronation Cars were introduced which brought innovations such as heating and doors, but the rise in popularity of the more flexible bus meant time was running out and the last tram ran in September 1962.

ABERDEEN

The history of Aberdeen's trams began in 1877 with the introduction of horse-drawn carriages. Electric power was then used until 1958 when the cars were disposed of by being burnt at the city's beachfront.

DUNDEE

Dundee's trams went as far as Monifeith and Broughty Ferry. They ended operations in 1956 and, like in Aberdeen, all the cars were burnt.

BUSES

The bus has served rural and urban passengers throughout Scotland and in 2014–15 there were 414 million local bus journeys, serviced by more than 200 bus companies. While more environmentally friendly buses have been introduced, the experience for the passenger has changed little over the years.

C'mon and get aff (Come on and get off)
**APOCRYPHAL SAYING BY GLASGOW BUS CONDUCTORS
TO PASSENGERS SLOW TO DISMOUNT**

DID YOU KNOW?

The most northerly bus stop in Scotland is on Unst in Shetland. As befitting its special status, it has been suitably furnished with curtains, comfy seats and a carpet.

AVIATION

From its early days, there has been considerable interest in aviation in Scotland. The first air show in Scotland, at Lanark in 1910, brought a quarter of a million people to see the latest aeroplanes and when Concorde made its last appearance in Scottish skies in 2003 the roads around Edinburgh Airport were crowded with those keen to see a last glimpse of this iconic airliner, an example of which is a major attraction at the National Museum of Flight in East Lothian.

THE FIRST FLIGHT

The first-ever flight in Britain took place on 27 August 1784 when Edinburgh chemist James Tytler ascended in a hot-air balloon. He took off from the Holyrood area and floated over the city for a short time before coming to land in nearby Restalrig.

FIRSTS ACROSS THE ATLANTIC

It was a Scot who navigated the first non-stop flight across the Atlantic. In June 1919 Glaswegian Arthur Whitten Brown directed his pilot John Alcock from Newfoundland to their landing in Clifden in western Ireland. The first east to west aerial crossing of the Atlantic was by the R34 airship which took off from East Fortune airfield in East Lothian on 2 July 1919. Its crew were feted on their arrival in New York before making the return journey.

BARRA

The airport on the Outer Hebridean island of Barra is unique in world aviation: it is on a beach. Arrival times are dependent on the tides at Traigh Mhòr.

EVEREST

It was two Scots who piloted the first flight over the world's highest mountain. David McIntyre and Douglas Douglas-Hamilton flew two Westland Wallace biplanes over Mount Everest in April 1933.

DID YOU KNOW?

The shortest commercial flight in the world is between Papa Westray and Westray, two of the Orkney islands. The journey takes less than 2 minutes.

SHIPS

Scotland's difficult terrain meant that it was natural for ships to be used. Scottish burghs needed ships to carry their goods to market and armies found they could travel far quicker by sea than on land.

Before the major bridges were built, travellers used ferries if they wished to get from the Lothians to Fife, and then from Fife to Dundee without going on a long detour. The Fifies – the ferries between Fife and Dundee – ran until 1966, when the Road Bridge opened.

Scotland's islands still depend on their ferry services. The Corran Ferry takes cars across Loch Linnhe, 9 miles south of Fort William, on a journey that lasts just 10 minutes. Much bigger boats operate on the major routes in the Firth of Clyde, to and from the Inner and Outer Hebrides and to Shetland and Orkney. The main operator is Caledonian MacBrayne. Ferries from Cairnryan connect Scotland to Northern Ireland. (An ambitious Victorian plan to build a tunnel between Ireland and Scotland never got under the ground.)

RESOURCES

WEBSITES

University of Glasgow http://www.gla.ac.uk

The Glasgow Story http://www.theglasgowstory.com

Undiscovered Scotland http://www.undiscoveredscotland.co.uk

National Archives of Scotland http://www.nas.gov.uk

Scran http://www.scran.ac.uk

National Library of Scotland http://digital.nls.uk

Historic Environment Scotland Heritage http://portal.
   historicenvironment.scot

Oxford Dictionary of National Biography http://www.
   oxforddnb.com

English Heritage http://www.english-heritage.org.uk

Antonine Wall http://www.antoninewall.org

McGonagall Online http://www.mcgonagall-online.org.uk

Orkneyjar http://www.orkneyjar.com

Oxford Reference http://www.oxfordreference.com

Burns Country http://www.robertburns.org

Dictionary of the Scots Language http://www.dsl.ac.uk

Scottish Natural Heritage http://www.snh.org.uk

Northern Lighthouse Board https://www.nlb.org.uk
Gazetteer for Scotland http://www.scottish-places.info/
Scottish Brewing http://www.scottishbrewing.com

SELECTED BIBLIOGRAPHY

Buchan, James *Capital of the Mind: How Edinburgh Changed the World* (John Murray, 2004)

Croft Dickinson, W. and Duncan, Archibald A. M. *Scotland from the Earliest Times to 1603* (OUP, 1977, third edition)

Crofton, Ian *A Dictionary of Scottish Phrase and Fable* (Birlinn, 2012)

Forsyth, Roddy *The Only Game: The Scots and World Football* (Mainstream, 1990)

MacIvor, Iain *Edinburgh Castle* (B. T. Batsford, 1993)

Lynch, Michael *The Oxford Companion to Scottish History* (OUP, 2007)

Maclean, Fitzroy *Scotland: A Concise History* (Thames & Hudson, 2000, second revised edition)

Royle, Trevor *Culloden: Scotland's Last Battle and the Forging of the British Empire* (Hachette, 2016)

Goring, Rosemary *Scotland: The Autobiography: 2,000 years of Scottish History by Those Who Saw It Happen* (Penguin, 2014)

Watson, Fiona *Pocket Giants: Robert the Bruce* (The History Press, 2014)

ACKNOWLEDGEMENTS

Thanks go to Neil Fraser, Sandy Buchanan and Conal Anderson for insights and examples into how you are 'here to enjoy yourself'; to Rachel Dowle for Shetland knowledge; to Jean Walsh for her generosity in adding colour (and facts) into a dry and sketchy outline; and to R. A. and H. B. Ferguson for a lifelong interest in the country. Special mention goes to my family for the chance to see the country anew. Special thanks go to Nicola Sturgeon, Cameron McNeish, Ian Rankin and Professor Hugh Pennington for taking the time and trouble to answer my questions on their Scotland. This book would not be possible without the enjoyable professionalism of Summersdale's Claire Plimmer, Robert Drew, Sophie Martin and Imogen Palmer.

SNOWBALL ORANGES

One Mallorcan Winter

PETER KERR

SNOWBALL ORANGES
One Mallorcan Winter

Peter Kerr

ISBN: 978-1-78685-042-3

Paperback

£9.99

When the Kerr family leave Scotland to grow oranges on the island of Mallorca they are surprised to be greeted by the same freezing weather they thought they had left behind. They then realise that their new orange farm is a bit of a lemon... *Snowball Oranges* is hilarious, revealing and full of life and colour, set against the breathtaking beauty of the Mediterranean.

'This should do for Spain what A Year in Provence *did for France.'*
THE SUNDAY POST magazine

'Kerr writes with a combination of nice observation and gentle humour.'
THE SUNDAY TIMES

KNOWLEDGE

STUFF YOU OUGHT TO KNOW

RAY HAMILTON

KNOWLEDGE
Stuff You Ought to Know

Ray Hamilton

ISBN: 978-1-84953-889-3

£7.99

Hardback

This outrageously informative book is packed full of fascinating nuggets of history, science, literature, technology, sports, geography, culture and miscellanea from every corner of the world – enough mind-blowing trivia to ensure you're never short of a jaw-dropping conversation starter (or stopper) again.

If you're interested in finding out more about our books,
find us on Facebook at **Summersdale Publishers** and
follow us on Twitter at **@Summersdale**.

www.summersdale.com